Ask the Experts

Ask the Experts

*The Unique Benefits of Working
with Top Professionals*

Eszylfie Taylor
Vanessa Terzian
Dana Dattola
Monty Kennedy
Brian Parsons
Charles G. Stanislawski

CONTENTS

PREFACE

Why You Need to Work with
Top Professionals and How to Choose Them

The world is a different place than it was before the financial crisis of 2007. Yes, the economy has recovered for the most part, and the vast majority of industries are back on track and doing well, but things are different now.

Professionals in industries ranging from finance to real estate have lost trust and credibility. People feel like they were hoodwinked, had the blinds pulled over their eyes, or, worst of all, were intentionally deceived. Scores of homebuyers are now dealing with ballooning interest rates because they were sold on initial "teasers," or loan balances, that are now skyrocketing.

Many people still believe that these professionals are to blame for their financial woes. Sure, the homeowner signed on the dotted line, but it's hard to argue that the language in these contracts can be difficult to tackle, at best. The over-optimism and blind pursuit of the almighty dollar by some of these once-trusted professionals led them to bulldoze many innocent bystanders.

Deserved or not, this distrust still looms large in the minds (and wallets) of most consumers. People don't know whom to trust or which direction to turn.

From the financial industry to the real estate industry, it seems that everyone is saying something different. Consumers are being told to do away with hiring a professional and take matters into their own hands.

The danger with consumers not working with professionals is that many people have never been exposed to the necessary information to make educated decisions. If you think you are going to read one book and become knowledgeable enough to manage your financial future, you might want to consider the time and learning curve involved in mastering the industry.

There is a lot of conflicting information about how to get your financial house in order, navigate the real estate market, plan for retirement, and more.

Although it might seem like the days of trusting other human beings, even though they might be a licensed professional, are long gone, there is actually a light at the end of the tunnel—a chance for reconciliation. The government is implementing new laws designed to restore trust in the consumer/professional relationship and make transactions more consumer-friendly.

Take, for instance, the 2010 Dodd–Frank Wall Street Reform and Consumer Protection Act, a federal financial law that went into effect on October 3, 2015. This law aims to simplify the loan terms in government-mandated forms such as mortgage interest rates and prepayment penalties. The law also requires that consumers see the final contract terms at least three business days before closing, an effort to ensure that they have time to understand what they're agreeing to.

With any major change or implementation such as this, some professionals or industries will be more prepared than others will. During this time of mending, what you absolutely don't want is another professional who is ill-equipped, ill-prepared, or uninterested in keeping up with the latest developments to serve your needs.

How do you select professionals in any industry who know current laws? How do you avoid those who haven't taken the initiative to take classes or catch up on all the new rules?

Now, perhaps more than ever before, there is a great need for referrals or introductions from trusted professionals. But in these fickle times, the search can't end there. Due diligence must be done on the part of the individuals to ensure that they're getting involved with a qualified, standup professional.

What are the due diligences that must be taken? How do you decide whom to hire to manage your finances, your legacy, and your family's future? How do you choose someone to help you acquire a large asset, to buy a home, or to expand your portfolio? Mortgage broker or a bank? Real estate planner or a CPA (certified public accountant)? Agent or team? These are difficult questions for difficult times.

You will learn the answers to all those questions in this book.

The chapters will introduce top professionals, who they are, and what they do. We will cover many important topics, such as:

- The difference between working with a bank instead of a broker.
- The benefits of hiring a real estate team instead of working with an individual Realtor.
- Why you need business insurance if you are an investor or contractor.
- The biggest misconception that consumers have about having a solid financial foundation.
- Why you need an estate-planning attorney instead of a CPA.
- How working with a team to build your financial house can save you time, headaches, and possibly money.

Plus, you will learn what to look for in these professionals and what aspects are most important.

It's normal for a family or individual to have a family dentist, the same pediatrician for 18 years, or even a lifelong gardener; but how many people have a team of financial professionals that they consult when they need advice? You might think a team of professionals is unnecessary because you're not a six-figure earner, or you rely on your employer to tell you what to do with your 401(k). Or maybe you do have a high income but are unprepared for an emergency or unexpected situation, such as divorce, a lawsuit, or an accident, and quickly find yourself scurrying to find professional help.

The reality is that you need an entire team, from the moment you are born to the moment you leave this earth. You need an estate-planning attorney, because estate planning isn't only about death; it's about protecting those you love. Whether you have $50,000 in retirement or $1.5 million, it needs to be put to the best use. Instead of stressing to find a professional right away, start now to build a relationship with your personal professional, so when you're ready to buy or sell a home, set up a will, or make any other important move, you know who to call.

Ask the Experts relies on an army of trusted advisors, suggested to you by the best professionals in the industry. With this resource, you'll be prepared for whatever life throws your way.

INTRODUCTION

Every day we deal with people who think they are "all set" and we always ask them, "What does that mean?" Most people have made at least the basic strides in planning their finances. They're participating in a retirement account, or they have insurance, or they have done some kind of preparation; but it's usually far from what they should be doing. The sooner they recognize the deficiency, the sooner they can rectify the issue and get on track to reach their goals.

Today's economy is unpredictable, and market returns are not doing what they've done in the past; with pressures on social programs and an ever-diminishing set of business owners who offer pension plans (which most working people relied on previously), there's a greater onus today for people to take charge of their own financial affairs to make sure that their houses are in order. There is a need for people to be educated and to have the information to make the best-educated decisions for their own financial well-being.

The average consumer is generally ill-equipped to learn the differences among insurance options, investments, and planning tools. *Ask the Experts* is a resource to help everyone get his or her financial affairs in order and prepare for the future.

Many people are stuck on issues of avoidance or procrastination when it comes to their financial security. It seems too complicated or too time-consuming. Most people simply don't have the confidence, and do not feel empowered to make the best financial decisions for their needs. It is like trying to drink from a fire hydrant; there's more coming at you than you can ever take in.

So, it is important to focus on what is relevant to your life, to take that first step to seek out the resources that you will find within these pages. With the right guidance and information, you can become empowered to plan your financial future and make the decisions that are right for your needs.

The biggest difference between these resources and other options is that professionals avoid making absolute statements. Too many teachers and programs will say, "Everyone should do this," or "Everyone should buy this," and "No one should ever do this." Yet, no one should feel compelled to do, buy, or avoid any option without understanding his or her decisions. You should do what makes sense for you, based on your needs, timelines, and objectives.

There are pros and cons to each product and decision, and once you have learned what the options are and the benefits and drawbacks to each, you are intelligent enough to evaluate the potential outcomes and make the right choice. You should never follow a program blindly, but should seek out a basic understanding of what your goals are and which resources and actions are going to help you achieve them.

Many successful people become so focused on what they're doing in the present, on the issues directly in front of them, that they tend to put off financial planning. By demystifying the plans, ideas, and concepts available to the average consumer, professionals empower you to focus on your long-term goals. It isn't about how much experience you have with money, but what you know about financial planning that matters. You need to know the basic principles, with respect to each area, that make up your financial portfolio.

The information in this book is as applicable to a 25-year-old as it is to a 75-year-old. It is applicable to anyone who is seeking to get his or her financial health in order. However, it is certainly best applied in the building phase of life, rather than at the preservation or exit point. This information will help someone in the accumulation phase of his or her financial timeline.

Those who have successfully accumulated some wealth, or who are prepared to experience some level of success, will benefit most from this information. These are the people who have something to protect, who are prepared to buy property, or who have the means to make excellent financial decisions with access to the right information and financial planning education.

The expert professionals in this book hope to raise consumer confidence and financial literacy in the general public. People who only do one or two things to secure their financial outlook are typically not educated about the options and are often paralyzed by fear from taking further steps to better their financial end. Others may blindly make choices that are based on generalized advice, even though they don't fully understand the details or the process.

It is important to dispel the myths surrounding money matters because there are pros and cons to everything. Professionals can overcome misinformation by explaining exactly what each option consists of, alongside the benefits and drawbacks to each choice.

You can find plenty of resources to explain why life insurance is good and necessary, if that's what you're looking for. But there are plenty of other sources that will tell you why life insurance is a rip off, if that's what you're looking for. Whatever information you seek, you are bound to find. Yet, if you start from a neutral point and focus on learning and understanding the actual positive and negative points of each option, then you are empowered to decide on your own.

Advisors should be facilitators of your needs, not dictators. Yet, you have to have some foundation to start from and the ability to articulate your needs. The expert interviews in this book will give you the foundation and ability to identify and seek the solutions that are going to help you succeed.

FINANCIAL FOUNDATION

What Does It Really Take to Have a Solid Financial Foundation?

"Knowledge, without application, is useless."

Interview with Eszylfie Taylor

Eszylfie Taylor is a financial advisor who focuses on creating a solid financial foundation by describing his experiences with a wide cross-section of clientele. He has worked with a variety of professional athletes, entertainers, business owners, doctors, lawyers, real estate professionals, and others.

Eszylfie works hard to help his clients feel empowered with the objective of demystifying the complexities of insurance and financial planning. For more than 17 years, he has been focusing on his clients' objectives while providing what they need to meet their own financial goals.

Holding the firm belief that knowledge is power, and that knowledge without application is useless, Taylor helps his clients avoid ever having to say, "I wish I would have known that," or "I didn't know that's how it works." He offers a variety of financial planning strategies and explains the pros and cons of each. His ultimate goal is to have the greatest possible positive impact on his clients and others. He does this by ensuring that his clients have the proper tools to make informed choices for the benefit of their own futures.

In this interview, Eszylfie Taylor answers the common questions that many consumers share regarding the financial planning industry, and how they can benefit from more information and more options. While average consumers are successful and capable, it is their understanding of financial matters, and their awareness of the available options that can make the difference between financial success and financial ruin.

I help my clients prepare for the calamity, that if something should happen and they did not come home to their family tomorrow, or lived until age 100, and everything that could occur in between. Many people don't know what will become of their families if they should unexpectedly pass away. These are the challenges and hurdles that Taylor addresses with his clients, all while ensuring that they learn how to make their money work for them.

What do your clients have in common?

The most common thread between my clientele is that everyone has achieved some level of success and prominence in his or her own right. There is immense variance between professional focus, ethnicity, and background; but success is one thing that my clients have in common.

How would you define your role in your industry?

I am a financial advisor. My practice is comprised both of the asset protection side and the investment advisory side. This means that we do a lot of insurance for asset protection, including life insurance, disability, long-term care, and so on. Then, we have the investment advisory practice, focusing on mutual funds, stocks, bonds, annuities, and alternative investments.

Concerning financial matters, do you feel that consumers are knowledgeable?

I think that most people are intelligent and capable of grasping financial planning concepts. However, I also think that when it comes to financial literacy, as a whole, the average consumer is a novice. This is, in large part, because they were never really taught such things in school. People often shy away from making difficult financial decisions because they haven't been prepared for or exposed to certain things.

On the other hand, some people will jump in head first, making poor choices because they haven't been given the information to make educated decisions.

That's why I love what I do, giving people the information that they need to make informed decisions. I tell them the pros and cons of planning concepts, products, and ideas. I empower the consumer to make wise financial choices.

Do you find that most consumers have a solid financial foundation and are prepared for emergencies, unexpected situations, and retirement planning?

I think the majority of people are either ill-prepared or completely unprepared. I would say that nine out of ten average consumers are not prepared. Most are just one or two paychecks away from complete financial ruin. I always tell people that it doesn't matter what you make, because it all comes down to how much you keep. The average consumers are more than capable of making good decisions and setting themselves up accordingly. It's not a lack of aptitude, but a lack of exposure and education that makes them ill-prepared.

What do you help your customers to achieve?

I'm not a salesperson; I'm a facilitator. I'm someone who asks people what they want, listens to what they say, and delivers. When they receive the information and help they're looking for, they can crystalize their goals and I can help them formulate an action plan. There are a lot of products out there, a lot of plans, and a lot of white noise. There's so much of this that if people simply said, "I want to understand everything there is to know about finance", it's like drinking from a gushing fire hydrant; there is far too much coming at you that can possibly be consumed.

That's why it's better to ask, "What's applicable to my life? What are my objectives? What are the things I should know, based on where I am in my life today and where I want to be?" This really narrows the scope down to what's relevant, making it much simpler to grasp the options and products that make the most sense for the individual, and go from there.

What outcomes do you help clients avoid?

When it comes to avoiding poor financial outcomes, I want to eliminate statements like, "I wish I would have known that," or "I wish someone had explained that to me," or "I didn't know that's how it works." These are the common phrases and statements that I want to avoid for my clients. Whether they do something or don't do something, I want it to be of their own volition, fully understanding the pros and cons of their decisions.

That is when my job is done, when I can say that I've educated my clients. It is up to them to buy today or not, but if I have educated them on the options, I've done my job.

What are the major benefits of working with you to achieve a successful outcome?

The benefit of working with me in my practice is that we take a macro perspective. This means that I'm not a product seller, but I am a problem solver. I work to understand the entire scope of my clients' situations before making recommendations.

Experience is another major benefit. I've been in the business for more than 17 years, and I've seen a lot of clients in a wide variety of situations. I have learned from the things that those clients have done well and the things that they have done poorly. I can use this experience for the benefit of my clients and help them avoid pitfalls and mistakes that could set them back.

I often use my own life as an example. I've achieved a great deal of professional success, but I've also endured a lot of needless failures, simply because I didn't know any better. My parents told me to work hard and save. Those are good principles, but where and how do you exercise them? Nobody told me where to save, how to save, how to invest, or how to buy real estate. Those are things that I've had to learn the hard way.

It is one thing to be given these general principles for success in life; it is another for them to be a bit more granular and in depth. It's important to say, "Here are the things you actually want to look at." Otherwise, even if you run hard, you could be running in the wrong direction and find out far too late.

What led you to this field?

I enjoy helping people. I also enjoy finance, planning, and affecting change in people's lives. This is what drew me to this field and after 17 years, I can say that I never imagined what a positive impact my work would have on people's lives and the community, at large. I didn't fully grasp the impact that I would have when I started.

The work that I do helps people keep their mortgages paid, fund their children's college tuitions, minimize taxes, and keep businesses open. These are all things that not only affect my life and my client's life, but they also affect their family's lives and everyone who is connected to them financially. It is much greater than I am. It will transcend and live beyond my own existence, a reverberation or a domino effect. There will be grandchildren and great-grandchildren from these clients who will benefit from the work I did with their ancestors. That's just powerful.

There's no specific story of how I chose this field, though. I think it's a general thing, because I sell an intangible good. I sell increased confidence. I sell this idea of financial security. I sell this concept of protection, but what does it look like? You can't show it off or put it in a trophy case, so it isn't tangible.

Now that I'm in the second half of my career, I can see how the promises I've made are coming to fruition and the impact that this has had on people's lives. People are retiring comfortably, sending their kids to college, selling their businesses, and finding that a life insurance policy has replaced someone's income.

To see these things happen—not just spoken of as a theory and not shown in someone's spreadsheet—to see the actual impact gives me a renewed sense of passion and vigor.

How and when did you get started in the business?

I started right out of college, when I was 22 years old. I wanted to be a millionaire by the time I was 25 years old, and I entered the business thinking that three years was enough time to reach that goal. What really drew me to the business at that time is that I would be paid, not for my age or tenure, but for my work ethic and productivity.

I love what I do, and since I graduated from college, I've known nothing else. I jokingly tell people not to ask me about fine dining or world travel or politics. That's not what I'm interested in. But if you have questions about finances, I can answer them.

What is the driving force that inspires you to help others?

At this point, it's about impact. I wear a bracelet that has the word "Impact." For me, success and money are good. We need money to live, be comfortable, and care for our families. However, at the end of the day, it all comes down to the impact and the mark that we leave in the lives of others.

That is my driving force; it's what motivates me the most. I'm able to build an organization and employ people and feed their families. With my clients, there are probably thousands that I've helped over my career, and it is amazing to see the impact and hear the stories about the work that I've done and how it has changed lives. The reverence and appreciation that people have for what I've done for them is great.

What is the biggest misconception that consumers have about having a solid financial foundation?

The biggest misconception is that being successful and making a lot of money makes you a good planner. Some of my wealthiest clients could pass you on the street, and you'd never know. Some clients have the nicest suits and a big fancy car, but they're living paycheck to paycheck.

The idea is that it's not what you make; it's what you keep. If you make a million dollars and spend one million dollars, you're just as broke as the next guy. You want to designate a portion of your income to savings and allow your money to work for you because one day you will not want to. The time to start is now.

In my estimation, the average consumer has a grave misconception of how much money they will need to accumulate to be financially secure. That's because they're not thinking about taxation, inflation, volatility, and risk. These are the things that I help them to think about and prepare for.

What's the biggest pitfall that clients aren't aware of?

Consider the analogy of Mount Everest. Mountain climbers dream of reaching the peak, so what do they do with that dream? They plan, train, take the necessary supplies, and then they go, just like consumers who are planning, training, eliminating debt, getting the kids out of the house, building businesses, saving retirement accounts, and so forth, retirement is their Mount Everest.

One day, that mountain climber will reach the peak of Mount Everest and say, "I did it." Consumers will pay off houses, save millions, reaching their financial goals as well. Interestingly enough, more people die each year descending Mount Everest than those who die on the way up. This is the same fate that befalls consumers. We are so concerned with reaching the top that we fail to consider the most important thing: the exit.

We fail again to consider the impact of inflation, market volatility, and how illness can affect our outlook. Much like building a house with a deck of cards, you can take painstaking efforts to build a masterpiece, but it is still fragile. In one fell swoop, without adequate stability and foundation, one slip of the wrist can undo years of hard work, sacrifice, and discipline.

I have an ideology of preservation and protection over simple accumulation because it's just as important to preserve and protect what you have as it is to grow it.

How can someone avoid making mistakes and being ill-prepared without a solid foundation?

I tell my clients that if you aim at nothing, you will hit it with amazing accuracy. Most people fail to have an action plan. They're living in the moment. They're working, taking care of their families, going to their jobs, saving, and trying to reach goals; but there is no exit plan. I help my clients avoid this calamity by reverse engineering. I want them to think about where they want to be in 30 or 40 years, the type of life they want to live, and what that will require; then, we simply reverse engineer. I build plans and structure things that put them in the right position to realize their own dreams.

Can you share an instance when you helped a customer in the past?

Every day, I deal with people who think they are "all set," and I always ask them, "What does that mean?" It's not that people haven't done anything; they're participating in retirement accounts or have some kind of insurance and they might have done some planning. Even the average consumer has done something, but it's far from what they should be doing, in totality. I think the important thing is getting people to recognize that they've done well in their planning thus far, but that they have more to do; there are other things to consider.

The sooner people recognize the deficiency and the sooner they can recognize the opportunity to improve things, the faster they can rectify the issue and get on the right track to reach their goals. When I started dating my wife, we were discussing plans. I told her I had set up college funds already, and she asked if I had kids. I said, "Not yet."

This is just a byproduct of me starting in this business so early. I saw the value of compounding interest and time and wanted to take full advantage of that.

I can also give you an example of estate planning. Based on current law, the exemption is about $5.4 million per person, and a lot of people don't recognize that if their estate is in excess of that threshold, the $5.4 million will be subject to a 40 percent progressive tax for their heirs.

There was one family I met, with an estate worth more than $30 million. They were feeling good about themselves in the work and the discipline that they'd put forth to reach that point. Yet, they had not recognized the deficiency in their plan.

They needed estate planning and insurance plans to offset the tax liabilities. Their children were looking at a $10 to $11 million tax, and most people's estates are comprised of what I call ill-liquid assets. That means business interest, real estate, and things like that. When these taxes are levied, the US Internal Revenue Service (IRS) takes cash. If your portfolio is comprised of real estate or business, you're going to have to sell it all, probably at a loss.

That's something your family has to bear. It's a keen example of planning that I was able to handle with one client, to establish an estate plan and purchase particular policies to pay the estate taxes at pennies on the dollar. It's an example that I use consistently with people who have millions, but don't realize that they have a deficiency in their plan.

We can definitely make the money. But, we are taxed when we make it, and we are taxed when it's gone. We are taxed when we pull it out, and again when we leave it to heirs, if we don't plan properly. That's one of the things that I'm trying to do: help clients plan properly and not have greater exposure than necessary. I help clients avoid greater and higher taxation.

What is your best piece of advice for someone who is considering getting a financial assessment?

My one piece of advice is to take into account all aspects of your financial well-being. If I have a financial advisor and he or she manages my stock portfolio, there are still other things to consider to ensure that my financial house is in order.

All the efforts of my financial advisor might be a tremendous resource in the arena of achieving financial security, but there is a necessity for proper planning with insurance investment and the assistance of tax and estate professionals.

What should someone look for in a financial advisor?

You should look for someone who takes a macro perspective and looks at everything. You want someone who has strategic relationships with other advisors and professionals, so they can work collectively. There's nothing worse than having a planning team comprised of attorneys, CPAs, and adversarial financial advisors. You want to have someone who has the client's best interests at heart and tries to do everything they can to put the client in the best position in the future. At the same time, you have to make sure that their ideologies are aligned with yours, and that they can collectively help you reach your goals.

What are the most important questions that someone should ask when seeking a financial advisor?

More important than the questions you ask, make sure that you are tuned in to what the advisor says and the questions that *they* ask. If you meet a financial advisor who immediately starts telling you to buy this, move this, or shift your assets here, you should walk away.

Think about seeing a doctor. If you walk in, and the doctor says they're going to schedule a surgery for tomorrow, without ever asking any questions or checking your records, you know you need to see a different doctor. It is the same with your finances. To find good financial advisors, you need to know about their experience, how long they've been in the business, and what their philosophy is when doing business with clients. These are the most important things. Ask yourself if the person represents you, or if he or she represents their company.

How can consumers learn more about creating a solid foundation while looking at their finances?

You want to have a keen understanding of your income and your expenses. I'd suggest that you map out what you have coming in, what you have going out, and the gap between discretionary income. I'd have a good budget outlined and copies of any insurance policies, investment accounts, or anything else that you've already established. There should be a full analysis to understand who you are, today, before taking any recommendations to purchase, move, or act in any way. I always tell clients that I will never undo any good work that they've done. If they have plans and have done things in the past that are sound and working toward meeting their objectives, I won't touch those things.

If there are ten things that the client needs to do to be financially secure, and they've already done seven, then I'll affirm those seven things. Then, I'm going to highlight those three errors of vulnerability and focus on solving those problems. That's the mark of a good advisor: If it's not broken, don't fix it. Focus on areas that are of concern and have not been addressed.

What is the most important thing that people can do to make sure they have all the protection they need for themselves, their family, and their legacy?

Start by asking yourself, "If I didn't come home tomorrow, what would happen to my family?" Then ask yourself, "If I live to be 100, can I sustain and maintain my standard of living?" Whether you don't come home tomorrow, or whether you live to be 100, anything can happen in between.

We want to make sure that we plan for these occurrences, any of which could happen. You need to know that if you don't come home tomorrow, your affairs are in order; and if you do live to 100, you can offset the prospects of running out of money, volatility, and illness that could derail your retirement.

People often are caught up in products and things more than delving into what they want to accomplish. There is no perfect

17

product. No one product or plan is going to be perfect, all by itself. There are pros and cons to everything, but through a well-balanced, mapped out, and diversified approach, you can create a perfect plan. The catch is then to keep up with the moving target, the changes of life and objectives.

The only certainty in life is uncertainty. I might have a client's seal of approval today, with all plans taken care of, and everything in a straight line. But, that might not be the case in five or ten years. You have to periodically revisit your plans.

Could you share another example of someone you've helped?

In the course of more than 17 years of experience, I've realized that there are three major economic downturns. One that comes to mind now is a case from the 2008 financial market crash. A client was in the clothing manufacturing business and was doing really well, making a lot of money. I happened to catch him at the right time and had him putting money away in different insurance plans and investments.

When the market turned, and a lot of his competitors went out of business, he almost lost his property. I remember a conversation where he told me how appreciative he was that I had taught him many concepts that helped him save in a way that saved his business.

As a result of that, I started going a step further when asking clients about their plans. I used to ask how much money they could comfortably set aside for the future. After the crash, I realized that I needed to ask how much they could comfortably set aside with a number that's both comfortable and meaningful. So, if they want to put $200 per month into their 401(k), I ask them if they're planning or saving for retirement. The answer is generally yes, and the amount they've chosen to invest is comfortable; but is it meaningful?

Is that sum of money, compounded over the next 20 years, going to be enough to replace your standard of living? A figure of $100 per month is comfortable, but when you retire with a check for $10,000; how much is that going to help? If you want a six-figure income for retirement, then investing $100 per month to that goal is not going to work. You have to invest something closer to $1,000 per month. It's important to realize, early on, that you still have time to let your money work for you.

How can a consumer find out more about what they need to do to become better educated about their finances?

Consumers should work and engage with someone who knows how to do the work right. I practice what I preach. Consumers can reach out to me at www.taylorinsfin.com. I'm licensed in more than 30 states, so I work with clients across the country. My particular practice is not a transactional firm, but a relationship-based firm. We focus on building relationships and long-standing meaningful interactions with clients. We're not trying to sell a product or set up a plan today, but to be here for the individuals at inception, through accumulation, and into the exit.

What are the pros and cons of working with large firms versus independent firms, like yours?

There are pros and cons to everything. When you work with a large firm, you have resources, which is good. The challenge is that the larger firms can be too generic and not as fluid and amenable for clients as smaller firms can be. Smaller firms can react more appropriately to the needs of their clients, and with fewer constraints. Yet, the smaller firms don't have the same resources, support, and infrastructure as larger firms. It's difficult to say whether one is better than the other. Ultimately, it comes down to the expertise and the relationship with the advisor, more than the size or name of the firm.

What is your favorite quote?

"Knowledge, without application, is useless." If you have been given these insights and have these tools available, but you don't use them, it's all wasted. Once you have been given these ideas and resources, you have to use them to achieve success.

Investing involves risk including the potential loss of principal. No investment strategy can guarantee a profit or protect against loss in periods of declining values. Past performance is no guarantee of future results. Please note that individual situations can vary. Therefore, the information presented here should only be relied upon when coordinated with individual professional advice.

BABY BOOMERS

Advice for Baby Boomers Who Are Caring for Aging Parents

"I feel like what I do gives people peace of mind.
I can assist with ensuring family relationships stay intact."

Interview with Vanessa Terzian

Ten thousand baby boomers (born between 1946 and 1964) retire every day. Couple that with the fact that these baby boomers have Millennial children (born 1980s–2000s) who are living at home longer than ever, and you can see the financial strain start to stretch thin.

Furthermore, factor in the fact that people are living longer than ever, and that these baby boomer retirees could also be taking care of themselves, their mid-to-late-20s children, and their 80-year-old-plus parents. In times like these, it's more important than ever for families to have the always difficult, "If I'm gone tomorrow," discussion.

Vanessa Terzian is an attorney specializing in estate planning. In essence, she helps people manage their family's assets as the elders age and become unable to make sound decisions on their own, and eventually when they pass away. She has clients more than 100 years old, some of whom are more mentally spry than their own 70-year-old children.

We all want to think that the worst won't happen to us. As humans, we're reactive by nature, but Terzian urges people to fight those fears and become proactive with their estate planning. It is essential to protect your family's wealth—not just the tangible wealth, but your legacy as well, to make sure everything you've worked for transcends to the next generation.

Do you know where your parents' records are? Do you know what would happen if the unspeakable occurs tomorrow? Do you know whom to contact or which financial professionals your parents have been working with?

In this interview, Terzian discusses several topics related to estate planning such as how to open the doors of communication among family members (because this is a subject no one likes to talk about), how to decide who will play key roles in the estate planning, where vital documents are located, where the assets are held, and how to avoid getting entangled in a fight with the state and probate.

Estate planning is different than it was 20 years ago. What challenges should I expect as I move forward with the process?

The biggest issue is that people don't realize that the documents and legal framework that they manage today will be important while they are still alive. They often say things like, "I don't need a will or a trust because I'll be dead and gone. I don't care what happens then." It's important to understand that these documents could be critical if you become incapacitated in some way while you're still alive, or even while facing the normal aging process.

What unique challenges do baby boomers face?

Millions of baby boomers are retiring every day, and many are either ill-prepared for it, or they are facing the natural problems that come with aging. It's taking longer for kids to get through college and get out on their own, so this age group is supporting both their kids and their parents.

Just recently, a customer said to me, "I need to change my trust because my sons are 27 and 29, and they still live with me. They haven't found their way in life yet. If they suddenly receive assets and money and funds, they're not sophisticated enough to handle that. They haven't been on their own yet." She actually changed the age at which the assets would be distributed to her sons to 40 years old. It might seem strange, but she had to consider whether they would be able to manage the assets if something were to happen to her tomorrow, and she just didn't feel comfortable with the answer.

Do you feel like most estate holders have properly prepared their estates, in case of crisis?

I do not think that people are innately proactive. They tend to be more reactive, and it's difficult to talk about those things, so I like to give people tips and ideas on how to begin this conversation with their aging parents.

Specifically, what value do you bring to families? How do you help them?

Ideally, I open the doors of communication among family members to discuss what would happen if and when these triggering events take place. For example, if you were incapacitated tomorrow, what would happen to your kids, and what would happen to you? How do you want decisions to be made? The more detail with which we discuss these concerns, the better prepared you're going to be.

I want to make sure that the legal framework and documents are in place. From there, I start talking to the people who will play those key roles in drawing up your estate-planning documents so that they are prepared when that moment comes. They need to know where the documents are located, where the assets are, and all the ins-and-outs of the next steps.

With so many statements being electronic these days, many people don't get anything in the mail and have little idea of what their parents have or where they have it. Sometimes, tax season will come around, and the family will start receiving 1099s from accounts they didn't know existed. So, the first thing is to ensure that the right documents are in place. The second thing is to implement an action plan for key people to handle those documents, when the time comes.

In the same vein, what disasters do you help families avoid?

The biggest outcome that I help people avoid is going to court. My goal in arranging these documents is to ensure that your family never has to walk into a courtroom or deal with the court process. In Los Angeles County, the process is a lengthy one, because all our local probate courts were consolidated into one courthouse in downtown LA about three summers ago. The entire county of LA is in one single courtroom. It is an emotionally draining, lengthy, and costly process.

My next goal is to help families avoid disputes. I don't want to see anyone's family torn apart over who got Mom or Dad's wedding bands, for example. I want them to know what to do when the time comes, so they're not feeling uncertain. I want them to preserve, or even improve, family relations by discussing these issues, ahead of time.

How will working with you, in particular, make me more successful in this area of my life?

I understand that when it comes to achieving successful outcomes, there is no tool more impactful than the family meeting. No matter how beautiful the set of documents, if the plan isn't implemented, it doesn't work, and you've wasted your time and money. If everyone is clear on their role, then the plan flows much more smoothly.

I tell my clients, "You're stuck with me for life," and I really mean that. This plan needs to be reviewed at least every three to six years. Because the family meeting is part of the flat fee that we charge for our estate-planning process, it is the best way that I can ensure the plan will actually work.

My time at Wells Fargo as a trust administrator gave me a clear, solid understanding of the different family dynamics at play. I feel strongly about my ability to help people achieve their desired results while maintaining family cohesion.

What led you to becoming an estate-planning professional?

I came into it a little bit by accident. I didn't know exactly what I wanted to do. I was among the youngest students in my class, I graduated early, and I went to law school from there, without really thinking much about it. I just knew I wasn't ready for the real world, so I stayed in school. Law school seemed like a good choice, and I was fortunate to find an area that I loved. And I met my husband there. We practice together, so that was a nice outcome of a difficult three years of law school.

I was recruited out of law school by Wells Fargo's trust department, and that threw me into administering about 320 trusts at a time. That was a great hands-on learning experience in how trusts work, but also how they don't work when they're not properly drafted or maintained. I did that for several years before working for a private law firm, and then going out on my own about seven years ago.

I find this area is great for women. If you have your own firm, you have some flexible hours, but it also has an emotional and relationship-based side. As women, we listen well, we can work with families, and we appreciate the emotions that are tied to these legal documents. I think it was perfect for me in that regard, so I got lucky.

Why are you passionate about this?

The most common comment that I get from clients after we've proactively discussed and completed our estate plan is, "I am so happy. This feels so good. I have peace of mind." I'm proud that what I do gives people that peace of mind and allows them to live life with the knowledge that their loved ones will be taken care of, no matter what happens to them. What I do relieves a real burden.

Do you see families making any recurring mistakes concerning their estates, even before a parent becomes incapacitated?

The biggest mistake that I see people make is reacting to problems instead of being proactive in their communication and preparation. We all know that bad things happen, and we need to make a concerted effort to talk about it. Otherwise, people try to make decisions once they're in crisis mode, and that never ends well.

Another common mistake is that people assume that because they have seen an attorney at some point in the past, they have an estate plan in place. They put the information on a shelf, it collects years of dust, and they have no idea what it says; they don't remember. The people they've named as key players and decision makers for their finances and health don't stay in one place forever, so when the time comes, they have little recollection of who these people were, if they even still have the same job, or if they're even alive.

What is the difference between a will and a trust?

That's a good question, because it's a common misconception that a trust and a will are the same. However, while both are quite basic, they play two different roles. A will dictates where you want your assets to go and who will be in charge, but that's where it stops. A trust can do the same thing, but it carries more weight. It tells us who would be in charge during periods of incapacity, and it exists the moment that you set it up, as opposed to a will, which goes into effect only after you are deceased.

The other major difference is probate laws. Every state is different, but in California, if you own assets that haven't passed through a beneficiary designation, meaning you didn't specify "transfer on death" or "payable on death to beneficiary with a bank account," then it's an aggregate. If all the aggregate assets together are in excess of $150,000, the will is probated, meaning that the court defines the size of the estate. Many people think that if they have a will, they will avoid probate or that they don't have enough money to have a trust. But the threshold is only $150,000.

What major myth about wills do people believe to their detriment?

Many people assume that they will, by default, automatically inherit their parents' or spouse's assets, but that's simply not true. There are some common ways that you can jointly hold a title and put beneficiaries on accounts in order to possibly avoid probate. There are, however, some downfalls to that strategy, outside the "default plan."

The problem with the "default" plan is that nobody is officially in charge when you need someone to make medical and financial decisions, if you suffer a stroke, for example. You need to have proactively nominated someone in the legal documents, like a power of attorney and a health care directive, because nothing will be automatic. Probate, upon someone's passing, is the expensive legal process that you have to go through if you don't have a will or if you have assets in excess of $150,000.

What is the biggest misconception that baby boomers have about taking care of their aging parents?

The biggest misconception is that we all like to think our parents are invincible, especially our moms. They took care of us, and we don't think about having to care for them. We also don't think about the costs associated with that care. We think that we'll just be able to jump in when we're needed, but what happens if you get sick or hurt while your parent needs you? A lot of people also don't realize that it's not safe, as someone who is not a trained caregiver, to take on the tasks necessary to care for aging parents. At the same time, you're juggling your own career and family, and you need to be able to make the medical and financial decisions with the help of caregivers.

So, we know we need to talk about all these things, but what should we do if we don't know how to bring them up?

One way to initiate the conversation, if you have taken care of these issues yourself already, is to let your parents know that you have already gone through the process and can also help them through it. You might start with, "Hey, I just finished my estate plan. Have you guys done that?"

Then, you can ask, "Who are the key role players in your plan, and are they prepared?" If your parents are receptive, you can ask about where the documents are, and create a list of documents, banks, safety deposit boxes, location of their keys, and other practical and proactive things like that.

You can then discuss what sort of decisions they might want you to make with their finances or health care, and find out who will be supporting you at that time, who the CPA, the attorney, and financial advisors are. You can even meet these people to get a better understanding of how things will play out when it's time for you to become a part of that team to care for your parents. You can find out if they'd rather stay at home for as long as possible, or if they'd be happy in a nice community that provides ongoing care.

Of course, the end-of-life decisions are the most difficult to talk about. There are major documents you need to discuss on that end, such as an advanced health care directive that authorizes someone to make medical decisions, and a living will to address end of life decisions, like whether to refuse life support. There used to be DNR (Do Not Resuscitate) orders. Now, we have POLST (Physician Orders for Life-Sustaining Treatment), which might state that you don't want to be resuscitated at all, or that you do, but only under specified circumstances.

Can you give an example of someone whose parent's passing was an even harder struggle, simply because they didn't have these things in place?

I recall a family that had absolutely no discussions regarding the estate and what steps to take after Dad passed away. I was brought in after the fact. There were three siblings, and one of them—the one I represented—was chosen as trustee. She was chosen because she runs the family business, the CEO of the company, and was quite detail oriented. She also worked with their dad a lot before he passed away. There was a brother and a sister, and all of them were in their early 70s. None of them had seen each other in more than 10 years, and they didn't communicate directly. They were hard to reach.

There was money to be distributed to everyone, but nobody had communicated what amounts anyone would receive, the specific assets in trust, or what everyone's expectations were. I had to get the grandkids involved. They had absolutely no relationship with their respective aunts and uncles.

There was a substantial amount of wealth in the family, but no one had made any plans as to what would happen with any of it. We had to start with a small family meeting so that everyone could understand what was in the trust, how the finances worked, and how the business was being run. They didn't know what was going on, so they imagined the worst.

What's the best way for people to be proactive about the costs of caring for aging parents?

Ideally, the parents would be working with someone like Eszylfie Taylor to plan proactively for themselves. By the time you're 70 and experiencing health issues, there's no insurance to put in place for care or long-term costs. For baby boomers who are preparing to care for their aging parents, starting the conversation is the best way to be proactive.

What consequences might people face as a result of failing to set up proper estate planning for themselves or their loved ones?

Without a doubt, the biggest consequence is having to face the financial and legal issues, having to go through the court process at a stressful time in life, when you're in crisis mode, without a plan.

Emotional stress affects different people in different ways. Some people want to get things done, and others are nearly incapacitated. Until it happens to you, you don't know how you'll react, so it's best to have it handled before it happens.

Can you tell us about a time when you were able to help a family, in a positive way, with estate planning?

There was an aging father who had the foresight to call a family meeting with me in order to discuss some pressing issues. Dad was of sound mind, but he knew he was getting older, so he proactively added his daughter as a co-trustee. This allowed her to begin familiarizing herself with the various properties in trust.

Dad had a sort of internship period with her. Then, shortly after the meeting, his health started to fail, and we had another proactive conversation before he went into the hospital. At that point, he felt comfortable enough to hand over the reins to his daughter.

Instead of waiting for something to happen to him and having everything decided for him, he controlled the conversation while he was still able to. Now he needs 24/7 care and is in his late 90s, unable to keep things running as he did before. Rather, with a solid plan, he is receiving the care he needs, and his daughter is managing his affairs.

What is the best advice that you can give to baby boomers who have living parents, whether they are sick or not?

Communication is the most important thing. You have to communicate with your parents. There are many tips for communicating effectively and proactive ways to start conversations, so do your homework and quickly have these important discussions.

It is essential to be aware of the warning signs that elderly parents are aging, and to never assume that everything is okay. We get calls around the holidays after people visit their parents and notice a pile of unopened mail, expired milk in the refrigerator, and a strange smell in the house. They are signs common to typical aging, and this might be the time to start talking about things. But in reality, the conversation should start well before then. You don't want to jump to the conclusion that you need to take over for your parents, but you do need to start talking, no matter how uncomfortable it might be.

You might even notice that new people are becoming involved in your parents' lives. This is when people become vulnerable to financial elder abuse. It is sad to say, but the abuse is rampant. If you notice new people in your parents' lives, you need to look into it, start the conversation, and don't assume that people are behaving innocently.

How can baby boomers find out more? What's the next step?

The Internet is a great resource for information, but there are endless resources besides the Internet. Nonetheless, it helps to have some trusted websites to visit with lots of good information. Some examples are CareGivingAnswers.com, EstatePlanning.com, or Tanner.org.

At the end of the day, it's more about finding good advisors, which is why this book, *Ask the Experts,* is so important. You need to have a team in place because these are not one-size-fits-all issues. Online solutions related to estate planning can be misleading because you need personalized solutions for the specific details of your life.

INSURANCE CHECK-UP

The Importance of an
Annual Insurance Check-Up

"My first priority is to assist clients in identifying their exposures to loss, basically answering the question, What can go wrong?"

Interview with Dana Dattola

The primary goal of insurance of any kind is to protect an individual during an unforeseeable event such as an accident, earthquake, unfortunate passing of a loved one, or even a workplace-related incident.

The need for insurance grows every day in our constantly changing legal landscape. The Internet has ushered in a new age with even more exposures, and recent laws and bills regarding sexual preferences and equality for all have led to more discrimination and sexual harassment lawsuits. In short, there are simply too many unknowns to go uninsured.

According to Harvard Law School, the United States has the most lawsuits filed, the most judges, and most lawyers per capita in the world. As crazy as it sounds, sources say there is a new lawsuit every two seconds in the United States, and one lawsuit for every 12 adults.

This couldn't be truer in a highly litigious state like California. Dana Dattola is an insurance broker at Weaver and Associates in Los Angeles. In this interview, she will share insights on areas for which people might not have considered needing insurance.

Over the course of her career, Dattola has helped countless individuals and businesses avoid liability, risk, and property loss, saving them thousands of dollars in the process and further expanding their insurance education.

From house helpers to a pool in the backyard, there are blind spots with regard to insurance that many people aren't aware of. Even hiring an accountant for a small business requires insurance in case an employee is injured while driving to an appointment. Most people do not review their policies annually even though there are changes in their business and life that can leave them open for lawsuits. Dattola has solutions for these instances and more.

How does your company, Weaver and Associates, help business clients with their insurance needs?

We help business owners protect their companies and their families from four categories of risk: liability, property, personnel, and income. We do this through a systematic three-step process, designed to increase our client's profitability while lowering their exposure to loss.

What type of business owners do you usually help?

Our typical client is a business with 10–200 employees in which the business owner is still actively involved in the operations of the organization. We take a holistic approach to managing risks, which works best when we get to know and understand the ownership of a business and can assist with all the personal and business issues. The most common industries we work with include manufacturers, retail establishments, hospitality, contractors, and property owners. We also have some niche programs for import/export and nonprofit businesses.

What types of insurance do you offer to individual clients?

For individuals, we offer home and automobile insurance, in addition to personal umbrella policies. We also cover polices to protect boats, motorcycles, recreational vehicles, motor homes, secondary homes, rental properties, and everything else that matters to the client. Some examples of other important items include fine arts, jewelry, and other similar possessions. We also provide liability or workers' compensation insurance to protect in-house help, such as nannies, house cleaners, gardeners, and personal chefs. We can provide policies to protect against natural disasters such as earthquakes and floods.

Why do businesses need insurance?

Every business owner works hard to build their business, but they could lose everything in a moment with a single claim. It is important to remove their risk of losing everything by properly insuring businesses from liability or property loss.

What types of losses can a business experience?

As I mentioned earlier, there are four primary types of losses that business owners can face: liability, property, personnel, and income. Most of the time, business owners aren't aware of all the potential risks associated with their business. In order to identify the potential losses in a business, we work through step one of our three-step process called the Weaver I.M.T. Step one is identification where we identify every exposure (regardless of whether or not it is insurable) using our thorough risk analysis questionnaire.

What types of losses can an individual experience?

For individuals, the exposures are the same, except we substitute "personal" for "personnel," making the focuses liability, property, personal, and income. There's an exposure to property loss because a house can burn down, or a car can be totaled in an accident. There's also a significant exposure to liability, as the individual can be sued or held responsible for injuries that occur on their property. Even accidentally hitting someone with a grocery cart at the store carries personal liability, and there are insurance options to cover that. Personal losses would be things such as sickness, death, or disability. Income losses are a result of any of the first three, disrupting or completely destroying an individual's income and/or assets.

What challenges do you notice that business owners face when it comes to having or not having business insurance?

Rarely do I come across a business without any insurance in place, but it is common to find inadequate or incorrectly written policies. We have increased our minimum recommended liability limits to keep up with rising claims costs. Where a $1,000,000 liability coverage limit would have been sufficient in the past, it might not be enough to protect the business today.

We're also seeing a lot more claims for issues people didn't think about 10 to 15 years ago. For example, there are concerns regarding lawsuits for discrimination, sexual harassment, not getting breaks, and things of that nature. There's also the issue of cyber liability. If you have a restaurant with a point of sale machine, and somebody hacks into that machine to steal credit card information, there is a new exposure there that didn't exist 10 years ago. There are always new areas of losses and insurance policies to cover them.

What are the differences in coverage needs between a multimillion-dollar corporation with 50 to 500 employees and a small entity, like a tutoring business?

It is almost more important for small businesses to understand the exposures and adequately protect themselves than a large business due to the impact a single claim could make. A huge corporation might be able to self-insure in the event of one loss and might avoid total ruin, where a smaller business could not.

In the past, individuals and businesses didn't have as many considerations for risk protection as they do now. What do you think changed that has made insurance more important?

Technology is changing and opening businesses to new exposures. At the same time, attorneys are finding new loopholes and exposures to sue businesses.

Social changes can also increase business liability. For example, 20 or 30 years ago, you wouldn't have seen the high number of discrimination and sexual harassment claims that we see today. In the past, such issues were tolerated in the workplace, but today, they are not acceptable.

What outcomes do you help your individual and business clients to achieve?

We work to educate our clients to understand the exposures that they have to risk, along with the insurance coverage options that are available. We also address risk-management options that go beyond insurance. We want our clients to understand where they could have a loss and how to address that, regardless of whether the solution is purchasing insurance.

How do you provide that information?

Through the Weaver I.M.T. Step one is to identify the exposures a business faces; step two is to manage those exposures through risk-management processes such as safety training and implementing procedures and protocols; and step three is risk transfer or transferring of risks to an insurance company.

What outcomes do you help your clients to avoid?

Our ultimate goal is to help our clients make educated decisions. We never try to force anyone to buy insurance for the express purpose of simply having it or to make a sale. Rather, we are looking to really educate the client to make decisions. Some people might assume more risk than others, and there are different levels of risk that different clients are willing to take. In this way, we try to help our clients avoid having any losses. We don't want claims to happen in the first place; but if they do, we want the client to be protected and made whole again.

What is one major benefit of working with you to achieve the necessary protection?

The major benefit of working with Weaver and Associates is our proprietary three-step Weaver I.M.T. annual process. Many people buy insurance for themselves or for their business, and then they forget about it. Inflation and changes in laws and exposure make it important to annually review your policy. You might have some changes in operations in your home, or you might hire new people in your business. You might have layoffs or a new sector of business that opens you up to new exposures.

In your home, you might have added a swimming pool or a trampoline, and those items create new liability exposures. You might simply be holding church meetings in your living room that could create new liabilities you haven't considered. A lot of agents don't do an annual review, but these potential new exposures make the annual review process extremely important.

Is insurance always the best option for every client?

Insurance is not always the best option, and our goal is not to simply convince people to buy more insurance. A lot of people don't want to sit down with an agent because they think they are just going to be upsold. Our philosophy is to educate clients to make the right decisions for their needs. In some cases, this won't be to purchase more insurance. For example, a client might benefit more from self-insuring or simply minimizing their exposure. Instead of focusing on making a sale and adding more coverage, we focus on the various options that we provide our clients in order to minimize their exposure.

What led you to this field?

I am the third generation in our family's agency, so I grew up doing it. Initially out of college, I didn't want to do insurance because I just wanted to do my own thing. Then, I realized that I enjoyed insurance and already knew so much about it, that this is the industry I'd rather be in. It was fun to take over and start working with the family business. I ended up here because I like interacting with different individuals and businesses, and I feel like I'm helping protect what is most important to them.

They say in the insurance industry that you're either born into it or you fall into it. Nobody really wakes up and says, "When I grow up, I want to be an insurance broker." I am here to continue the family legacy. We've been successful for close to 60 years, and I want to continue that and have a place that my kids can one day take over.

What drives your passion to help people?

I am passionate about providing education to help people. Insurance can be complicated, and people often think that they don't need to know about it; they all just have it. Some will simply agree with the insurance broker and buy the recommended policy without really understanding what it covers or what exposures are present. Our goal is to put it all into non-technical language, so that our clients can understand what they're buying and what all the unfamiliar terms mean. I want clients to feel confident in their decisions.

There are different options when it comes to choosing an insurance company; so how can business owners decide whether to work with a company like yours or with a different sort of insurance company?

My strongest recommendation is to find an agent with a willingness to explain the products they are selling, as well as their process for identifying every exposure an individual or business might have.

Insurance is a competitive industry. Any agent worth talking to will have similar markets and products available. The key is to find someone you are comfortable with and who has your best interests at heart.

What is a common mistake that business owners make with regard to deciding whether or not they need business insurance and what type of insurance they require?

One mistake I see often with business owners who don't carry workers' compensation to cover employee injuries is that they don't think they need it because all their employees are 1099 independent contractors. However, if one of the independent contractors were to be injured on the business owner's premises or in their work duties, the courts will typically rule in favor of the employee.

You'll see examples of this in consulting firms, attorneys' offices, CPA offices, and other professional offices. A business owner might have all the CPAs as 1099 independent contractors to save the owner from having to deal with payroll issues. Yet, if one of those CPAs were injured while driving to visit a client, an attorney could find that they were acting more as an employee than as a 1099 independent contractor. Then, the employer could be held responsible for the injuries. It is a common mistake for these professional organizations to not have the workers' compensation insurance policy that would protect them from independent contractor injuries.

Another common mistake is that a lot of business owners don't have employment practices liability insurance (EPLI). This is a policy that covers claims from employees and third parties (like customers) for discrimination, wrongful termination, hourly wage issues, not getting breaks, sexual harassment, and other things of that nature. More often than not, the claim will come after an employee has been let go, and it might be retaliation. There's no coverage under workers' compensation or general liability for situations like this so having EPLI is important.

What is a common mistake that individuals make with regard to whether or not they need insurance and what type they should have?

The most common mistake that I see with individual clients is having minimal limits on automobile liability insurance. Cars are becoming more expensive, and there are state required minimum limits, which are too low to contribute much in an accident.

Another common mistake is not carrying renters insurance, when you don't own a home. Typically, renters don't see the value because they associate the insurance with just protecting their personal property. Yes, it does that, but many people don't realize that a renter's policy also provides you with personal liability protection, both at and away from home. A renter's policy can be as inexpensive as $150 per year and provides you protection if your dog were to bite someone while at the park, or if you were to accidentally injure someone with a shopping cart at the grocery store.

The last mistake we see is not carrying an umbrella insurance policy. This is a stand-alone insurance policy that extends both your auto and personal liability. An umbrella steps in after you have exhausted the limits on your auto or home/renters policy. Our opinion is that everyone benefits from an umbrella insurance policy but if you have any of the following exposures, you NEED one: (1) young drivers in the home; (2) a pool or trampoline; (3) more than $1,000,000 net worth; or (4) a dog, or other pet that could potentially injure others.

What is the biggest misconception about your industry that you find with business owners?

The biggest misconception about insurance brokers and agents is that we only want to sell you something. Many see insurance agents in the light of a sleazy used car salesperson. This is not how our office operates. A good insurance broker is going to try to educate you about your options.

What is your best piece of advice to encourage business owners to annually review their exposures?

Our annual review usually only takes an hour and that hour could save you hundreds of hours of time and plenty of resources if you have unidentified exposures. I really encourage business owners to sit down with a broker who is not focused on making a sale, but instead wants to help you to protect yourself against losses. Just as it is important to get an annual physical checkup with a doctor, it is important to get an annual physical checkup for your business.

What is your best piece of advice to encourage individuals to sit down and do the annual review?

I would advise individuals and businesses to set a date on their calendar for their annual review and stick to it. You'll benefit from identifying your risks and coverage needs and evaluating what might have changed over time. If you bought a home 25 years ago and never reviewed your insurance policy, it would be much more expensive to rebuild your home today than it was 25 years ago, and the dwelling limit on your homeowner's policy should be adjusted to reflect that.

What is the first step for anyone who is interested in learning more about obtaining insurance?

The first step is to contact an independent broker or agent. Don't ask for a quote to match what you have right now because you might not have adequate limits. You don't want to ask a new agent to copy a bad policy. Rather, you should start from scratch and take the time to focus on your needs.

What should people look for in an insurance broker?

You should look for a broker who wants to teach and is prepared to take the time to explain the options. Don't trust someone who wants to copy your current quote. Work with someone who is going to review your current needs and make sure that you have the coverage you require. It is also best to work with someone who can represent multiple insurance companies to find the best quote.

Why might someone choose not to obtain insurance?

There is a common mentality that nothing bad is ever going to happen to you. Hopefully, it doesn't, but you'll sleep easier at night if you know that you're protected if something does happen. If you go without insurance, you're rolling the dice and gambling on protecting what's important to you.

What are some questions that a business owner could ask while shopping for a good insurance company?

You should ask what the risk management process looks like. You should also ask how the agents determine coverage for each risk, how they feel about examining exposures in depth, and whether they are always available to answer questions.

How can someone learn more about insurance and about agencies like Weaver and Associates?

You can find an independent agent on the national Trusted Choice website (trustedchoice.com), which lists independent agents. You can learn more about Weaver and Associates by visiting our website (weaverinsurance.com) or giving us a call. You can even walk in if you're in the Camino Real, California, area; we'd love to meet you and pour you a good cup of coffee.

HOME PURCHASE LOAN

Navigating the Process of Obtaining a Home Purchase Loan

*"I have a passion for helping people, and
home mortgage loans happen to be my vehicle for doing that."*

Interview with Monty Kennedy

There are seemingly endless options when considering a lender for your home purchase. There are mortgage lenders and mortgage bankers, and there are different benefits of working with each. Still, this is a good time to buy; buyers in the market today have much greater confidence since the mortgage meltdown and don't have to fear predatory lending, as many people suffered and experienced in the past. New laws, such as the 2010 Dodd-Frank Wall Street Reform and Consumer Protection Act, ensure lenders are removing fine print from complicated documents in an effort to promote consumer-friendly language.

As home buyers re-enter the market, many have concerns because of previous bankruptcies, foreclosures, and poor credit. Monty Kennedy is a home mortgage lending professional who helps homeowners feel confident in the process and actually enjoy home ownership. Finding a lender who has been in the market through its ups and downs is important. You want a lending professional who can educate you, not only on obtaining the best loan, but also on helping you determine other important considerations such as evaluating whether you should put the full 20 percent down on a home, or if you should consider putting down less money to prepare for ancillary costs. Speaking of, what are ancillary costs?

In this interview, Kennedy, a lending professional with 30 years of experience, discusses the importance of hiring someone in his field who will be your advocate, who will educate you on the process and your overall financial situation, and who will give you advice on things like your credit card and debt-to-income ratio.

In short, Kennedy's main objective is to help people achieve the "American dream" of home ownership. He is your guide throughout the entire home buying process, helping you make the best decisions for your specific needs. A home represents a future. Kennedy helps you realize that future.

What are some of the challenges that you see with mortgages in the real estate industry?

Real estate has gone through a dynamic number of changes during the past several years. Fortunately, we're in a much better place than we were five to ten years ago. However, there are challenges, most of those being related to inventory. There's a lot of pent-up demand, and people who want to buy homes across the country find that buyer's demand exceeds the supply or availability of homes.

Some of the frustrations are really related to the reform that we've seen and the fact that there have been some changes and an overhaul in lending. At the end of the day, it's so we don't experience some of the things that we have in the past as far as the housing industry crisis was concerned. All in all, we're in a terrific place and I believe it's an incredibly wonderful time for people to be investing in a home, whether they purchase for the purpose of a place to live, or as an investment tool for them to leverage and build on as a foundation for personal wealth.

Why is it such a great time to buy right now?

Historically speaking, I think that we're still in one of the greatest times for homeownership. Certainly, from a cost standpoint, when you consider where interest rates are today, they're still incredibly low.

You've probably heard it said that real estate is a great investment. For many, it's a vehicle for not only accumulating wealth, but, in some circumstances, it creates exponential benefits. For example, there's the ability to have some tax deductions, which can make a critical difference for some people. Homes often work as a silent savings account of sorts, and that's big too.

I still own a home in Texas, and a large part of the reason why my wife and I still own it is because we see it as a vehicle, maybe even passive in a sense, that we can, at a later date, leverage and use for other big expenses. For example, we can use it to fund or partially fund college educations for our two children. There's a multitude of benefits of home ownership. What I love and have a passion for is educating people and being a resource and a coach to them, opening their eyes beyond just the thought of having a place to live. There are so many other potential benefits to consider.

What is the biggest change within the past five years that has had a positive effect on those who want to purchase a home?

There are a lot of positives. I think that we're in a better place as far as the quality of the loan products that are available and the commitment to educating consumers. We really go above and beyond in the measures we take to educate home buyers, from day one, about the process of purchasing a home and getting a loan. In the past, people would get a loan without fully understanding what it involves.

Today, we work with clients to review things like credit history, income, assets, and things of that nature. There is a little more of a gauntlet to the process today than previously. We have a more substantial process in a lot of ways. It is a great opportunity for people to educate themselves about the process and give sincere, considerate thought to the purchase. We help support people in financial literacy and help them make good financial decisions.

When I'm working with clients, there's far more to it than just figuring out what they would qualify for or what home price they could possibly obtain and purchase. It is equally important, if not more so, to discuss things like budgeting and their real comfort level for a monthly payment. What is the payment that they're going to be comfortable paying each month? How long do they want to own the home? Are they aware that interest accrues over time and that there are benefits to making additional principal payments, or paying off the loan early? In today's market, there is a higher quality of education and knowledge for clients and homebuyers.

What do you offer your clients as a home purchase professional?

My role is one of a teacher and an educator. Essentially, what I do in working with new clients or repeat clients is to get a sense of their goals and what it is that they're trying to accomplish. Then, I can educate them about the steps and the process that we'll be going through, together, in attaining that goal of home ownership. We review credit history, job history, income history, and determine where the comfort zone is in their monthly budget. We consider cash flow, budget for down payment, and the resources of the consumer.

Based on that dialogue and the relationship that we've developed through these conversations, I can then present my clients with options. I get a sense of people's preferences, needs, and financial picture. I help them to determine which possible mortgage solution works best for them, and then help them to make that decision. Once we've met all the requirements from a lending perspective and from their perspective in that financial decision, that's when the magic happens. That's when they get the keys to that new home, which represents so many different things for them, including their futures. That's what I get fired up about—making that positive difference, having a positive impact on people's lives. Home lending happens to be the vehicle that allows me to do that.

What market do you work with?

I primarily work with, and on behalf of, people who are interested in purchasing single-family homes, that being either one single unit or up to four units. These are people who have an intention of buying that home to live in, or as an investment property that they're going to leverage and rent out.

Beyond that, I have several passions, as far as specific niches. I really like to work with a variety of people, and anyone with a desire to own a home is a good candidate for me to work with, whether they are first-time home buyers or seasoned investors. That goes back to my passions for education, teaching, and helping people make good decisions for themselves.

That's a big part of it for me. It's an opportunity to go deep and get to know people so I can get a sense of what their goals are in the short term, the midterm, and the long term. I open their eyes a bit to what the home represents for them and the potential difference that it can make in their lives. I show them the opportunity to build equity and create a foundation for building wealth and financial strength.

I also enjoy working with people who are going through changes in life. They might be in a similar place as I am with a new child or a few young kids, and they're outgrowing their home. It's time to move up and find a bigger place. It's always exciting to help people accomplish that goal.

Then, there are the folks who are downsizing and have found themselves to be empty nesters. Maybe their current home is a little more upkeep and a little more room than what they need, so they're ready to make that next move to a smaller home or condo. There are a variety of needs out there.

Another major passion that I have is each and every opportunity that I get to work for a veteran of our armed forces or someone who is actively serving in our military. If I had to pick one particular segment of clients that I have the most passion for, it is our veteran community. I think that there's no group more deserving of high level services of accomplishing that American dream of home ownership.

I find that real estate professionals often perceive a much greater level of complexity with US Department of Veterans Affairs (VA) home loans than actually exists. It's rewarding for me to help other professionals gain a higher level of understanding regarding the details and requirements of VA home loans. I enjoy being a voice of reason, truth, and education, so veterans can utilize an outstanding benefit they've earned.

What outcomes, aside from obtaining a home, do you help your clients to achieve?

Often, people purchase a home and then realize that there are a lot of other things that they need help with. For example, they need to think about insuring themselves, even beyond home insurance, and explore other insurance opportunities, such as life insurance, estate planning, and things of that nature. New home buyers might have had simpler taxes in the past, though owning a home and advancing in their career can make the tax picture a little more complicated. I help them make the right connections with various professionals for those needs too.

What kind of outcomes do you help your clients to avoid?

When it comes to helping them avoid the pitfalls of home ownership, it's important to make sure that the client is aware of the other services and things that can be put in place to protect themselves, their assets, and their goals.

I never want clients to get into a mortgage that they're not comfortable with. I help them to avoid getting into too large a mortgage payment and help them to prepare for additional expenses. People often qualify for a larger mortgage than they are actually comfortable with, so I help them to remain disciplined with the amount they are financially able to manage.

What led you to this field?

I have always had a passion for sales and interaction with clients. I've worked primarily in the lending industry since I graduated from college. I think the passion that I have for people, and that consistent and constant need for people to be able to leverage financing or lending services, created a perfect marriage for my interests. My passion for real estate, lending, and people is what ultimately drew me to this profession.

I was also drawn by remembering when I was younger and in a position to take on loans, like my first car loan or credit card, and I realized that a lot of those decisions were made without a whole lot of education or consideration. I wanted to be different from the norm and combine my passions for real estate, people, and education to make sure that people make their decisions with their eyes wide open, completely understanding all the details of the choices they make.

What is the most common challenge for someone looking to get a residential mortgage, even with good credit?

A lot of the challenges that people mention are only perceived challenges. There's a perception that loans are hard to get, that you have to have a perfect credit score or that you have to have 20 percent for a down payment. There are actually opportunities and solutions to help, which people aren't aware of. So, the biggest challenge is that people lack the necessary education about what's available. Too many people mistakenly believe that they're not in a position to buy a home. Even those who have faced previous foreclosures, short sales, or other adverse credit events can still buy a home.

For these people, I can come in and help develop a game plan. Depending on their individual situations, they might be eligible to buy a home through various available lending and mortgage solutions.

How can an experienced lender guide someone in the process of coming to the market to purchase a home?

If you're considering buying a home, it's critical that you work with an experienced lender, for many reasons. You want to get started on the right foot by working with someone who is offering realistic expectations.

An experienced lender starts the foundation for setting someone up for success, going deeper and doing more work upfront, and obtaining good data to work with. They can ensure that you have the conversation about income, assets, and what tax returns and historical earnings have looked like.

Working with an experienced lender helps people to avoid mistakes due to oversight. A good lender will fully vet and review the supporting documentation to offer great options.

How can someone who is looking to get a home mortgage avoid or overcome mistakes and obstacles?

I had a recent client who was excited to buy a home. He was talking with real estate professionals, viewing homes and everything, but he didn't think it was necessary to check into things like credit until after he found the right home.

His meeting with me was a great illustration of why being proactive regarding home financing is so critical. It turned out that the client had some previous issues with his credit. They were from years ago, but they were still on his credit report. It was an eye-opening moment, and it solidified the advice that I give to all my clients about getting ahead of things and being proactive.

I was able to guide this client with tips to help improve his credit. If he had waited until the last minute to address this, after accepting an offer and being under contract to start purchasing a home, then he would have had that additional stress of resolving the previous credit issue while also going through the process of buying a home, evaluating the home, and doing inspections.

What should someone think about when considering a mortgage banker or a mortgage broker?

With a mortgage banker, clients are choosing an institution to process their mortgage application. A representative of a mortgage banker, such as me, walks the loan through a set process. Many mortgage banks underwrite, approve, and fund loans in-house. The mortgage bank I work with also services the majority of the loans it originates, so my clients are sending their mortgage payment directly to the institution they chose to work with.

The mortgage broker community is a little bit different. A representative takes applications, prepares a loan package, then presents or sends it to several different lenders. Those lenders can then purchase that loan from them. This can be a great solution for people, but it can also have challenges.

There is a lack of borrower control through this process due to a dependence on people to do a good job and provide a high level of expertise, attention to detail, and commitment to service to meet your expectations. The uncertainties and lack of choice can be a challenge.

In some instances, there are additional requirements that have to be met when working with brokers. The further you get from the money or the initial lender, the more overlays, guidelines and requirements have to be met, making the process more involved, in many cases.

What should someone ask when interviewing a mortgage lender?

Regardless of who you're working with, you have to ensure that it's a good fit and that you have good rapport. Ask who you will be dealing with throughout the process. Will it be the same person who is helping you with the application or someone else? Ask if they will handle the processing of the loan file internally, if they underwrite and fund their own loans.

Find out if they work with the same people throughout the process, and ask who you will be making payments to after the loan is funded. Ask about the benefits in working with a mortgage broker or a direct lender. Find which lender would likely be a good fit and why. Finally, it's a must to know about the experience of the lender in handling, processing, and successfully closing home purchase loans. The market is competitive, and who you work with really matters.

What is your best piece of advice to those who are considering purchasing a home?

My best piece of advice is to call Monty Kennedy. Beyond that, educate yourself on the process, leverage resources, and leverage professionals. If you were going to have surgery, you'd want to meet and seek the counsel of medical professionals. You'd want to get feedback, advice, and a clear plan.

Similarly, if you want to successfully purchase a home and achieve all your goals, you want to speak to an experienced professional. Take action, reach out, and spend some time with an experienced lending professional to develop a game plan.

What's the first thing someone should do when they are ready to purchase a home?

The first step is to make an appointment and meet with a lender to provide advice and details about the process. Then, you can begin the application process for preapproval. Do the homework, start the process of preapproval, and know what you can reasonably and comfortably obtain and maintain in a home loan.

If someone has just started looking for a home, what advice can you give about the strategy of making an offer?

When it comes to home loans, structure is more important than price. You need to leverage the expertise of qualified real estate professionals. I tend to defer to the real estate agent professional in the process of determining a price.

I educate my clients to be aware of ancillary costs, which are expenses involved in, but not directly related to making a purchase. They need to calculate what changes they might want to make to the home, and be careful to avoid exhausting their resources without leaving a margin for the unknown. Just this month, I had a client who was sold on putting 10 percent down on a condo. I was able to give her a broader perspective just by asking questions like, "What do you think this particular condo is going to need to make it your home?"

She had several thoughts about it, but hadn't thought about the costs associated with those things. She hadn't thought about unexpected repairs or others needs that might arise. Even the costs associated with moving have to be considered, as they can be substantial.

Ultimately, this client chose to put down a 5 percent payment instead of 10 percent because she realized that 10 percent wouldn't put her in as comfortable a position to make the house a home.

How can consumers find out more about how to get approved for a home loan with you?

There are so many ways for people to reach out to me. I'm a people person, so I love the opportunity to speak with people and meet them face to face. To get the process and the conversation started, people can connect with me and keep up with me through resources like my website (https://www.homestreet.com/person/monty-kennedy), LinkedIn, and Facebook, not just to initiate the process of qualifying for a mortgage, but also to access information and educational tools.

I can't wait to pick up the phone or have that next client walk in the door and get started working with them on this journey of buying a home.

REAL ESTATE TEAM

Benefits of Choosing a Real Estate Team over an Individual Realtor

"My goal is my client's goal; I'm here to help."

Interview with Brian Parsons

Choosing a real estate agent is like choosing a good pair of shoes: you need a perfect fit from the start, you want to feel comfortable, and you want to feel satisfied that you chose the right one for your needs. When you're in the market for an agent, there are myriad questions you must ask yourself. "Do I want to work with an agent who juggles several listings at once? Would a solo agent have time to adequately market and sell my home? Where would it leave me if my Realtor goes on vacation or has an emergency?" When faced with the decision, should you hire a family friend or go with a referral from a different source? How important is it to have an experienced agent or team that specializes in representing a buyer or representing a seller? What if you overlook a major detail when making the transaction?

Between helping residential homeowners market their homes, searching for other sellers and buyers, communicating with escrow companies, coordinating with inspectors and vendors—all while providing excellent customer service and attention to detail—a solo agent has to divide his or her time among all these areas for each and every client.

The Parsons Team members realize the importance of providing each client with their full attention, so they created a team system to handle the different areas of a real estate transaction.

When you hire a team over an individual agent to sell your home, you don't pay any more than if you had used a solo agent.

Brian Parsons leads the Parsons Team of seasoned residential real estate professionals. Thirty years ago, Parsons' parents, also real estate agents, came to the seemingly obvious realization that two minds are better than one. Two opinions, two sets of expertise, and double the availability means that your agent never goes on vacation, never gets sick, and is never stumped for an answer because they have the support of a team behind them.

Today, Parsons has taken the reins from his parents and continues to deliver superior customer service to his clients using the team approach of helping clients buy and sell property.

In this interview, Brian shares inside information about the state of the real estate market in Los Angeles today, what homeowners should do to maximize their returns, and common pitfalls to avoid. He goes into detail about the do's and don'ts of buying and selling, including the repercussions of working with an agent who doesn't treat your case with the highest level of professionalism.

What is your real estate specialty?

I am in the residential real estate industry: townhomes, condos, single family homes, and residential income properties like duplexes and triplexes. We also specialize in new construction sales.

We've seen a lot of volatility in the housing market throughout the years. What is the market like now?

It's gotten a lot more complicated throughout the years. My mom's been in it for 33 years, and she used to tell me that there was only one page to sign when a house got new owners. Now, there is more concern about lawsuits, so we're seeing a lot more disclosures, a lot more paperwork.

People breeze through and sign the papers, because it's becoming too much to read. We need to sit down and go through disclosures, reports, and inspections with our clients, so they know exactly what they're signing. Paperwork has been a huge change in our market, but even still, the industry is doing great. The market is fabulous. We're currently in a seller's market with little inventory. If a house is priced right, we can sell it, and with multiple offers.

Since 2008, Pasadena has seen a 20–30 percent drop in business. Yet, we were lucky, because other parts of the country saw drops of 50 percent or more. We're fortunate to be in a neighborhood with higher incomes, close to downtown Los Angeles, and with a lot of old money.

On the lending side, financiers are being more cautious, which is a good thing because people need to make sure they can afford the house. We're not seeing a lot of foreclosures and short sales. This is good, because it means people aren't losing their homes, hurting their credit, and struggling with money.

How did the Parsons Team come to be?

My parents started the Parsons Team when they realized that one agent wasn't able to do everything. There are more than 50 people involved in each real estate transaction, and you can't give the best possible service to your client all on your own. The tasks involved include marketing the home, looking for other sellers and buyers, communicating with escrow companies, and coordinating with lenders and inspectors, all while taking excellent care of the client. This is why my mom started a team. She was one of the first real estate agents to have an assistant, then a buyer's agent, and finally a marketing manager. Now, the team consists of multiple agents who help one another succeed and provide the best possible care to each client.

What is your role on the Parsons Team?

I am a listing specialist and team leader, which means I focus on listings and getting the highest possible price for our clients. I don't work with buyers. I negotiate contracts and let the buyer's agents show the property.

I start with the beginning stages of getting the home ready, determining what the presentation of the home will look like. I evaluate whether it needs to be painted, staged, or prepared for professional photographs. I work with our listing manager to create brochures and marketing write-ups, let the neighbors know that the home is coming on the market, hold open houses, and share the information with other Realtors and buyers.

I let as many people as possible know that the home is heading to the market. People love talking about real estate, so if I tell one person about it, he or she is going to go to work talking about it. Technology is important, but word of mouth is, and has always been, the supreme marketing tactic.

Our listing manager handles a lot of the details, but I know how to price a home right, so that we can get multiple buyers and remain in control of the negotiations. If we get no buyers, then finally get an offer, that buyer is in control of negotiations. If we have multiple buyers, then we are in control of the process and can negotiate to get the seller more money in the long run. We work to get the highest price and to save money for our clients by having the buyer pay for certain things.

In addition to getting a good price on their properties, what other outcomes do you help sellers achieve?

A lot of people like to start projects on their house to get it ready to market and sell without talking to us first. However, if they don't know what projects to invest their money in for the greatest return, this can be a downfall. Huge makeovers aren't always necessary; simple things, such as a carpet change and a coat of paint, can make a huge difference.

There's something that my cousin calls "escrow flowers," which are the new flowers that we plant along a walkway before we list a property. I love that term. Little things, like that, make a huge difference in the first impression and curb appeal of a home. The front door of the home is another big one. If it isn't impeccable, it deserves to be cleaned, painted, or even replaced. A fresh front door creates the feeling that a potential buyer is walking into their next home.

Some people want to put on a whole new roof or redo the electricity or plumbing. These things don't add value for the buyer. Buyers purchase based on emotions, and emotions come from seeing the property. If potential buyers can't see the plumbing, the electrical work, or the new air conditioner or furnace, then the seller should pass on making these improvements.

The best ways a buyer can add value to a property are by painting, replacing the carpet, staging the home, improving the kitchen and bathrooms, and anything else that is significantly visually appealing. That's how they will get the biggest return on their investment. We help clients allocate money to the areas that will help them sell properties for more. If they take our advice, they save money instead of spending it in the wrong places.

My goal is to help them achieve their goal.

Besides spending money in the wrong places and not getting a return on their investment, what other outcomes do you help your clients to avoid?

We make sure that our clients don't end up in court. Like I said before, there's a lot of paperwork that accompanies a sale, and the industry ends up seeing lawsuits when certain information isn't disclosed. It's not usually intentional, but when someone doesn't think to disclose something, thinking it's not a big issue, this can be a problem for the buyer. You have to disclose absolutely everything. If someone has passed away on the property, you have to disclose that. If there are water leaks, you have to disclose that. Mold is a big issue right now. It's important to disclose everything you're aware of to avoid lawsuits.

So how will clients most benefit from working with you?

Our team knows the process, in and out. We know how to save sellers money, but ultimately, we know how to use technology to our advantage. At the same time, we haven't lost the personal touch. Real estate is still personal. Selling a home is an emotional transaction for people, so we're always there for our clients.

Even though we're Realtors, people often refer to us as psychologists. We hear it all the time. We're Realtors, but we're a shoulder to cry on. We see smiles. We see tears. We see it all. We have technology to send things electronically for signatures and things like that, but we're still here on a personal level. We know that our clients are people, and we don't lose sight of that.

How did you get started in real estate?

I used to work at a large amusement park as a recreation coordinator. I got paid the same as the coordinators next to me. I could go and work my tail off and make the best customer experience for our clients, and the person who came on staff after me could sit in his or her chair, do nothing, and still get paid. What I like about real estate is that I can go out there, help people, and be appropriately compensated for the service I provide.

I can remember times when we'd be on our way to a vacation, and my mom and dad would pull the car over to go into an open house. I never thought I'd be doing that, but now I'll be driving with my wife and pull over to check out a house. I didn't think I'd be a Realtor in the beginning. I started by answering phones as my mom's assistant. I did the bookkeeping. I was a buyer's agent. I had helped in different roles on the team, but I prefer the listing and selling side because, to me, it's the most rewarding. I get to really help people. I think a lot of agents just put up a sign and hope for a sale, but I feel that is unethical.

For me, it's rewarding to help the client get their home ready to list. It takes a while to get people to trust you because there are a lot of Realtors who are untrustworthy and unethical. It's interesting to be able to earn a client's trust when you show them how to get the house ready and move them through that process. It's rewarding. You're not friends in the beginning, unless it's a referral. We get a lot of people calling us just to ask for help. You become friends, because they grow to trust you. That's the most rewarding part for me, building those relationships.

What is the most common mistake that someone looking to sell a home is likely to make, when preparing to list their home and choosing a real estate agent?

The most common mistake is not asking a friend or family member for a referral. So many people have a real estate license, so everyone knows at least a handful of Realtors. People make the mistake of choosing their friends, instead of seeking a qualified referral.

Think about it like open-heart surgery. You can go to a doctor who's performed one or two surgeries, or you can go to a specialist who does it hundreds of times each year. You want to choose the experienced surgeons, because they know what they're doing. We know that selling a home isn't heart surgery, but it's financial surgery. If you don't know what you're doing, you can lose a lot of money.

What mistakes do people make when choosing between a single Realtor and a team?

The truth is, a single agent has a hard time handling all the details of selling a home. They need more than one client to feed their family, pay their taxes, and afford vacations. They can't survive on one client, so they're always out there looking for other clients. It's a lot of pressure.

A solo agent might not be able to properly market the home with online advertising, print advertising, coordinating with vendors, knocking on doors, and calling the neighborhood. They can't do everything that needs to be done to actually get the highest return on the property or the highest sale price, because they're out there showing properties and opening doors for buyers. Their main objective is to get more listings.

A single agent typically isn't focused on selling your home. Once they sign it, they hope another Realtor will do the work of actually selling it. We call this method the three Ps: Put it in the MLS (Multiple Listing Service); Put up a sign; Pray someone sells it.

This is an example of technology doing more harm than good. Once you put a home in our Multiple Listing Service, it gets distributed to tons of websites. Buyers can look for it themselves, but you still have to reach out to the Realtors to let them know what's special about the property and why you're asking that price.

You have to stay at the forefront of people's minds because there are hundreds of homes coming on the market each day, and you still have to stand out. That's why we call daily around the neighborhoods of our listings. My team and I call to personally tell people about the listing.

What do you find is the biggest misconception that sellers have about agents?

Clients often don't stray far from the three Ps; they tend to think that all Realtors simply put up a sign and the home sells.

That's not really how it works. There's a lot more activity involved. Our team is in the office every morning, calling agents, calling buyers. We have a fulltime inside sales agent. His entire job is to call around the neighborhood of a new listing to tell the neighbors about it. What we know is that within about a quarter mile to half a mile of our listings, there is somebody who knows someone who would love to be in that neighborhood. It's our job to find them. We hit the pavement, we're calling, and we're doing it all, just to make sure that the home sells.

When you sign a contract with us, we take it to heart. It says in the contract that we have to do our job to sell the home and get you the highest price. Our ethics align with that, so with every step forward, we keep that goal in mind. We don't operate on the hope that someone else will do the job for us.

On our team, my mom and I take the majority of the listings. We have a couple of buyer's agents, so they're out showing the property. We have an inside sales agent who is always on the phone. We have a fulltime listing manager who is doing all our appointment scheduling, as well as coordinating with photographers and vendors. She does the paperwork and manages our team.

Additionally, we have another assistant who is our marketing coordinator. She does all our advertising, making sure that our homes are promoted 24 hours a day, seven days a week. We have another person on top of that who does all the paperwork during escrow to ensure that we cross every t and dot every i. That allows the sales agents to focus on getting out there in the community to sell the property.

Are your fees different from those of other agents?

No, we charge the same fees that an individual real estate agent would charge.

How can a seller avoid or overcome a mistake to achieve a successful outcome?

I actually have a friend who was talking to me about selling his house. We were talking about price, and one day he called and said, "Brian, I really, really want to go with you, but my wife is making me go with our daughter's godmother."

I said, "That's fine. We're not here to get involved in family issues. If you have any questions or need me to do anything for you, I'm always here to help."

The agent they chose priced the home high. They dropped the price, then dropped it again, and still the house wasn't selling. He wanted out of the contract but the other agent wouldn't let him out. He called me and said, "Brian, I don't know what to do. We need to move. I have to get out of this house. I can't afford it. It's costing us too much money. I owe too much money. I'm struggling." He was basically breaking down. He said, "How do I get out of the contract?"

I had to tell him, "Unfortunately, you can't get out of these contracts. They're binding."

What I ended up doing was calling the Realtor to talk to her broker. I said, "Hey, if you guys let him out of the contract—obviously, you're not selling it, so you're most likely not going to get paid—so, if you let him out and let me take over, I'll pay you a referral fee." The referral fee is a portion of the commission, so they still get some compensation.

He's a friend of mine, so I didn't mind doing that. I wanted to make sure he was taken care of. There are a lot of television shows out there that show Realtors making a lot of money. There are a lot of costs for brokers involved in the selling of a property, so sometimes the money gets broken down into so many segments, and the work wasn't worth the profit. But he needed help, so we got him out of the contract and got his home prepared, something that the other agent didn't do.

We moved the furniture around, took pictures down, rearranged things, cleaned up, and took professional photos. It looked like the other agent just used a cell phone. It was subpar and unprofessional, with black-and-white fliers. We made nice, colored brochures. Everything makes a difference. If you walk into an open house and there are black-and-white brochures, the buyer thinks, "This is a cheap house." If you come in and have a nice brochure that's glossy and looks professional, it adds value. We did all of this for him, and the house sold within a week with multiple offers at the set price.

What are some of the consequences for someone looking to sell a home without an experienced professional and/or team?

Lost time, energy, and money. If an agent doesn't know how to negotiate or price a property the proper way, or how to get the home ready for the market, if they don't do the simple things that make the home visually appealing, then they're leaving tens of thousands of dollars on the table.

Can you recall a time when you helped someone navigate a difficult situation?

We deal with a lot of divorces, probates, and trusts. These are never easy tasks, because the people involved aren't happy; they're not talking. Or someone has passed away, and someone else might still be living in the property. These are all difficult scenarios, and they are interesting for us because we have to navigate communicating with each family member in a divorce, or three or four trustees involved in a trust. We become the psychologists again. We help them get through the difficult process of getting the home ready and then getting it sold.

What's your best piece of advice to someone looking to sell their home?

Do your homework on a Realtor. Look at a résumé and look for a track record. We always give our clients the option to call our last five clients. That way, they can speak to them and see what they have to say about us, and if we did everything that we promised. We're not going to give them our five best clients, but the last five transactions that we did.

What's the first step that a seller should take if they're ready to list their home?

We always tell people to ask for referrals from friends and family because those are going to be the best. I always recommend that people talk to three Realtors, because selling a home is so personal. So many scenarios come up that will require you to trust this person, so you need to interview three people. We're not always the right fit for everyone, but you need to know if we're a good fit for you or if there's a better Realtor who matches your style and personality. We always recommend talking to multiple agents to see what the options are.

Do you have a listing appointment process that sellers should know about if they're considering working with you?

Yes. We come out, take a look at the property, and get approval to look at the house, as a buyer. That means that I can come in and give you constructive criticism on the property and discuss how we can get it ready.

Sometimes, the sellers don't need to do anything. Sometimes, it's just coming in to take down personal photographs. We don't want personal photographs all over the place because buyers can get distracted looking at who lives there instead of getting emotionally attached to the property. We come in and do these types of things and go through our full marketing plan so they understand what we're going to do and what happens when we hit the market. We tell them about our open houses and our caravans for brokers to come by and take a look.

We discuss what the weekend will look like, what the timeframe is, and how we schedule showings. We go through the full process with each client. If we're not sure of the condition of the property before we arrive at the listing appointment, we set a second appointment to come back and go through the comparable sales. This helps us to properly price the home to get the most value out of it.

We're not just going to throw out a number and hope it works. We try to be more professional about it than that, so we come in prepared. If we're not sure of the condition of the home, we can come back and make sure that we run the numbers.

What types of considerations do you help the seller think about when considering pricing their home?

We look at comparable sales. If you have a single-family home, we want to look at other single family homes within a half mile or similar locations to yours. It's all about location, condition, and square footage. Is it a two-bedroom home? A three-bedroom home? We go through and find the best comparable sales that recently sold to see what the buyers in that marketplace are willing to pay.

A lot of people think that they can sell their home by themselves, and some people do have luck with that, but most don't. They are professionals in other areas. They might be a mechanic or a doctor. Their business is what they're good at, not selling homes. They might not know how to get the visibility and attract buyers, but that's where we specialize.

Our job is to go get them not just one buyer, not just two, but multiple buyers who are interested. What we typically see in a "for sale by owner" listing are several potential buyers who are investors, offering half the price or trying to get a good deal.

For sale by owners typically attract the wrong kind of buyers. They are people who aren't qualified to buy the property, and Realtors won't show the property, because we know we must do a lot of the work, the paperwork, the negotiating with a seller who doesn't understand the process. We're not taking our buyers to for sale by owner properties. We're going to take them somewhere else. If you're working with a Realtor, you're going to attract other Realtors, not just the buyers.

What should someone ask when considering an agent to help sell their home?

You should ask how many homes the agent sold last year. You should ask how many clients they're currently working with and how many they can handle. Ask for their list price-to-sales price ratio. Ask for third-party testimonials about their service.

Then, they should ask what the agent charges, what makes him or her stand out from the competition, and what they do differently. Ask what got the agent into the business. If they can't answer that question, then they're not excited about it; they're just there for the money.

How can someone looking to sell their home find out more about what they need to do first, before hiring an agent?

There's a tab on our website that tells you how to get ready to speak with a Realtor. Go to www.TheParsonsRealEstateTeam.com.

When someone decides to move forward with you, what are the next steps for the intake process?

It's simple. They'll sign a contract and get a phone call from my listing manager introducing herself. Though we have a team, I'm always the main contact. The listing manager helps and answers emails, and she is also always available to answer phone calls if I'm in a meeting. Then, we give the client a timeframe for when we'll take photos and stage the home, if that's what we're doing. We'll give a timeline of open houses and broker caravans, and we'll go from there and look at offers. That's the basic process.

TAXES

How to Reduce the Pain of Paying Taxes while Increasing the Possibility of a Tax Deduction

"The better our clients do, the better we do."

Interview with Charles Stanislawski

No matter whom you are, taxes are complicated. The rules and tax codes seem to change daily and the incentive to earn more is sometimes squelched by the knowledge that the more income you earn, the more the government can take away. If your approach to taxes is to look back at the previous year instead of planning ahead for the coming year, then how will you know whether you are overpaying your taxes?

Chuck Stanislawski is the owner of Stanislawski & Company, a certified public accounting and consulting firm that primarily provides tax accounting and business consulting services.

Stanislawski knows that the key to winning with taxes is finding the perfect strategy that will reduce your taxes and increase your cash flow, long before that dreaded April deadline.

A family owned business for more than 50 years, Stanislawski & Company works with both individuals and businesses, including nonprofits and trusts. With tax laws changing so much during the past decade, experienced tax experts are needed now more than ever.

Throughout the years, Stanislawski has helped his clients generate upwards of 700 percent return on investments. One client saved more than $2.3 million in taxes!

As a certified tax coach, Stanislawski constantly teaches his clients the crucial difference between tax preparation and tax planning - the latter being much more important, but often overlooked, component to tax savings. He compares it to putting off going to the doctor until you're really in pain, all the while, you're just getting worse. Stanislawski & Company helps clients avoid any pain in the first place, and ensures they remain financially healthy.

In this interview, Stanislawski shares information about the state of taxes, gives advice on how to avoid overpaying, and provides the initial steps toward tax peace of mind.

What is your role in the tax industry?

Primarily, I handle tax, accounting, and business consulting. In more than 50 years, I think my company has served almost every industry from medical, real estate, trucking, manufacturing, entertainment, sports, and advertising, to security, technology, financial services, legal services, auto dealers, and a lot more.

What challenges do consumers face with regard to their tax brackets and payments?

Due to the progressive tax rates, it seems that the more you make, the less you keep because the government keeps taking more and more taxes. The challenge is finding a legal tax reduction strategy to reduce your taxes which can directly increase your cash flow.

Do you specialize in individuals or businesses, or do you handle both?

Both, and you can add nonprofit organizations to the list. We also have almost a hundred different trusts and estates that we work with.

What is your company's history?

More than 50 years ago, my mom and dad started the firm and then I joined it after graduating from the University of Southern California (USC). In the mid-1980s, Dad retired and Mom passed away. Now, I get to carry on their tradition specializing in tax, accounting, and consulting.

Are people paying more today in taxes than past years?

Certainly. The government continues adding taxes. There's a plethora of new tax complications. It takes a computer just to figure out the tax, and more important, it then takes a tax expert to come up with ways to reduce that tax. Ten years ago, I could do tax returns so much more easily than I can today. There are more considerations now. You need a computer to even just calculate your tax liability, and then it takes an expert with decades of tax experience to look at the different scenarios and figure out ways to reduce that tax.

What led you into this field? Was it because you stepped into the family business?

My original plan was to be a pediatrician. But when I got to college, I took chemistry and I flunked it. Then I took accounting and I aced it, so the writing was on the wall. I started at Stanislawski & Company at age five as the executive sanitary engineer. In high school, I did a lot of copying and assembling of the tax returns. Then in college, I calculated the annual depreciation expense for hundreds of my dad's business clients. This was before computers, so we had to do the computations by hand.

What drives you to help people?

I thrive on creating tax reduction strategies that create more cash for my clients. My firm is a profit center, not an operating cost. Our motto is, "The better our clients do, the better we do." We saved one of our clients more than $2.3 million in taxes. Looking at a return on investment, some clients hope to earn 2 percent on investments, maybe even 5 percent. With some of my larger tax savings, my client's return on investment can be over 700 percent based on what they invested with my CPA firm and what we generated for them in tax savings.

So, there are CPAs, accountants, and tax preparers. Can you define the differences among the three?

The job of a CPA is to help you plan to reach financial goals. An accountant prepares and examines financial records. Tax preparers calculate, file, and sign income tax returns on behalf of businesses and individuals. What's really key here is that you want to get a great tax *planner,* because there's just so much more savings when you do a tax plan than when you do just tax preparation—what we call compliance work.

You are a certified tax coach. How is this certification different from a CPA or an accountant?

What I do is more of a sophisticated tax reduction strategy. I didn't get this until after 30 years of doing tax preparation. I thought I was really good going into the certification course. I said, "What are you going to teach me?" But I learned the more you know, the more you know you don't know.

What is the most common mistake individuals make when they file their taxes?

The most common mistake would have to be that most people don't understand the difference between tax preparation and tax planning. Tax preparation is filling out the right amount in the right boxes on the right tax forms - again, we refer to that as tax compliance. It's difficult to reduce your prior year taxes when preparing a prior year's tax return because the tax year is already over.

Tax planning is different. Tax planning is where you meet with your CPA to discuss your current year's taxes and come up with numerous tax reduction strategies, which you can implement immediately, and which will then reduce your current and future taxes.

Tax preparation has less value. Tax planning has a maximum value. Some people are more afraid of paying their CPA a tax planning fee than they are of paying 10 times that amount to the IRS! So the biggest mistake is that they're not asking for help. They are not consulting with their CPA, so they don't even know how much money they're losing. For instance, in the first hour or two with one of my clients, I noticed that the prior tax preparer wasn't attentive; I found $100,000 of errors! Had that individual never decided to see a specialist, he likely would have never known the last preparer had done a poor job.

Another way to put it, is that some people don't go to the doctor until they're really in pain, and yet their medical condition has gotten worse because of the delay. That's what it's like when a person changes their CPA too late. We picked up several new clients simply because the prior preparer was not doing a good job. We give a complimentary second opinion that identifies the differences between a tax preparer and a firm like Stanislawski & Company, which specializes in sophisticated tax planning.

What specific tax planning strategies could people use to improve their situations in the coming year?

One thing they can be proactive about is their estate tax planning, including setting up a living trust or will. This single action can save people thousands to tens of thousands of dollars in the long run. Now, there is a statutory fee that the estate has to pay to attorneys and executors, based on California statute, but if you have a trust, you can eliminate that.

I have a client who, unfortunately, was given poor advice about his estate. I had a feeling that things weren't right; the books from a partnership just seemed off. The problem was that the prior tax attorney had them gift more than 50 percent of the real property in a family partnership to the children who were partners. While it sounded like a great estate tax plan, it triggered the reassessment of property taxes. However, the kids didn't even know that they had this property transferred to them, so it wasn't a completed gift. I went back and reversed it, thereby eliminating the property tax increase of more than $80,000.

Fast-forward a couple of years, that piece of property was sold and when I looked at the books, there was some land value, and a building had been constructed and it was correctly capitalized.

However, I just didn't trust it, so I said, "Let me look at the escrow closing statement." We were unpleasantly surprised to see that the prior accountant never posted the original $2 million land purchase price. So, I was able to increase the cost basis of the property by more than $2 million, just before they sold it, thereby creating an extra $2 million in tax deductions, which ultimately saved approximately $1 million in taxes.

What are the benefits of having more than one professional working on your case?

I call it the team approach. You need a great financial advisor and you need a good banker. You need a good insurance person to cover you. You need a great CPA to do the books and the tax planning, a pension specialist, and a benefit specialist for all the medical plans for the employees. The goal here is to get the client to be a good listener and listen to his team members and their recommendations. Many times, the team can come up with great ideas together, because, you know, two heads are better than one. I have many clients, including family groups, who meet with their team on a regular basis to review what's going on with their company, their various entities, and their books. The team gives some great recommendations and we develop great strategies.

How can you help someone who owns a business reduce their tax liability?

The first step is to schedule a tax planning meeting and have new clients fill out a tax and financial plan questionnaire. I also review the past tax returns and then I develop a couple of tax reduction strategies, which, on the average, can save anywhere from $10,000 to $100,000 or more on taxes. Many people, the most successful, don't want help; they don't think they need it. That's where the challenge is, and it's why our initial meeting is free.

Why do you think they don't believe they need help?

When you look at the glass half-full, you only see the portion that's half-full. You don't see above the water line, and that's what we see. We see there's so much more there that could be full. It's what you don't see that's so important. It's what's *not* on your tax return that is so important.

Also, I've unfortunately heard people liken filing taxes to going to the dentist, because of the pain. It's certainly not a fun experience to sit there while we go through a full personal financial statement, the financial planning, the taxes, and detailed stuff. It's a major inconvenience, and people only do it because they have to. A lot of people have a gut feeling and realize they should get a second opinion and that's how we get our new clients. They think, "I don't think he's watching the ball. I think I'm paying too much in taxes." That's when we get the call.

How do your services help with real estate?

There's a lot of planning inside real estate. For example, the client I just told you about was looking at a complete reassessment of property taxes. Most people don't realize that even if it's a corporation or a partnership that owns real estate, and they change their ownership to more than 50 percent, it triggers the reassessment, even though there's been no change of title. There are thousands of real estate tax reduction strategies that could potentially be implemented, and every client is different. We've got a great QuickBooks template that we use for all our clients to set up all their real estate properties because it's the best way to keep track of two or more properties. With QuickBooks, all your financial information is in one place and easy to find when you're ready to file your tax return at the end of the year. Another advantage is if I've had my rentals for more than 30 years and I need to know which plumber fixed that particular property about five years ago so he can come fix it again, I can just look in QuickBooks and it tells me everything I need to know, down to the plumber's phone number. It's all your corporate history inside QuickBooks—it's a great way to help you manage your business.

How can you help someone with estate planning?

Our firm's been around for 50 years; we see a client or two pass away every month. My dad is elderly now, and all of his clients who started with Stanislawski & Company 50 years ago are also elderly. We do a lot of transitional planning and related estate tax planning. When people die, rarely do attorneys warn the surviving spouse about the rise in administrative work and costs. Whereas the client was used to filing one tax return every year, they now have to do two or three - one for the individual, one for the new trust, and one for the B trust and sometimes for the C trust. They're not told about the shock of the new filings and the associated costs. It's well worth the trouble, but it's important to have that heads-up. So, on the estate tax planning side, there's just so much that can be done to save in estate taxes and gift taxes.

I had a client who'd been with us for 40 years. His wife passed away, and then he passed away about a year later. When I worked on the estate tax return, it turns out this client gave $3 million worth of real estate to his children and never told us. We had not filed a gift tax return, and it generated over $1,000,000 in taxes, but with some sophisticated tax planning, we were able to reduce the million dollars to $300,000.

How can an individual avoid these mistakes to successfully achieve their outcome?

The mistake is when the client fears calling his CPA because he's afraid of the cost of a CPA instead of looking at it as an investment. A good CPA can get a return on investment—it's not 3 percent, it's not 5 percent; it's 100 percent, it's 500 percent, or 700 percent return on your money.

Look at it as an investment, almost like a business partner. Again, our motto is, "The better you do, the better we do." We are here to help, and if your accountant can't save you the equivalent of his or her fee in what you would have had to pay in taxes anyway, at the very least, then he or she is not doing a good enough job.

Are there any other impactful scenarios you'd like to share?

One was a referral from Eszylfie Taylor. We picked up a new business client who was a famous consultant for one of the Fortune 500 companies and through some sophisticated planning, we achieved more than $200,000 in tax savings. We set up a pension plan for him and we did some year-end bonuses to eliminate the double taxation. He was really glad to hear how he could reduce his taxes by more than $200,000, by simply listening to our tax plan. Eszylfie and I did that all within a week or two.

Some people who don't make a lot of money find it unnecessary to hire a tax professional. What would you say to them?

If the tax filing is simple with no tax issues, or if you have a W-2 and some interest dividends, then popular tax filing programs work great. We actually like the self-prepared tax filing programs for our clients' children because it teaches them how it works. Some of our happiest clients are those who came to us because they tried some of those tax filing programs, they input some of the information incorrectly and it generated an inaccurate tax return.

I actually have a couple of CPAs who tried doing tax returns on their own, and they're now with my firm, because they realized it is not as easy as it seems. If you have a normal, straight forward tax return, then the government 1040 is fairly easy. It's once you start receiving more income or looking for deductions on a house or receive an inheritance, that you need to seek the assistance of a professional. There's going to be trillions of dollars passing through to the next generation during the next couple of years, and we try to prepare our clients' children to be heirs to those fortunes.

What are questions someone should ask when they're seeking a tax professional?

When you look for someone, be sure to ask about their experience, training, and certifications. For example, my firm has CPAs, EAs (enrolled agent to represent taxpayers to the IRS), MBTs (master of business taxation) from USC and Golden Gate University, plus we have certificates from the Institute for Preparing Heirs and the American Institute of Certified Tax Coaches. As for other questions, you could ask for a couple of examples of tax savings that they've generated for their clients, and maybe even ask them for their clients' names to verify that their claims are accurate. Ask them what's the most money they have saved someone and how. Ask about their fees and how those work. Ask away, until you find the one who's at the top of the pyramid when it comes to tax specialization, accounting, and consulting.

What's your best piece of advice to avoid the pain of paying taxes?

When applicable, seek professional help. Realize you'll never know if you're overpaying taxes until you get a specialist to meet with you and go over your tax situation.

What would be your best piece of advice to someone who either does their taxes themselves, or they're working with another tax professional?

Two heads are better than one. It never hurts to get a free second opinion.

How can someone find out more about your company?

People can visit our website at www.stanislawskiandcompany.com.

ABOUT THE AUTHORS

Eszylfie Taylor

626 356-7637 etaylor@taylorinsfin.com

Eszylfie Taylor is the president and founder of Taylor Insurance and Financial Services located in the financial district of Pasadena, California, and serves as financial advisor to individuals, business owners, and high net worth families.

Over the past decade, Eszylfie has been widely recognized as one of the most accomplished producers in the industry, receiving the National Association of Insurance and Financial Advisors (NAIFA), "Agent of the Year award: Los Angeles" in 2010–2012. Additionally, Eszylfie is a 14–time "Million Dollar Round Table" qualifier, the last three of which he has been a "Top of the Table" producer and was the award recipient of the 2015 Top Four Under Forty Award by *Advisor Today* magazine.

Eszylfie has achieved consistent high levels of production due to a combination of education, motivation, a positive outlook, and a deep desire to help others improve their lives. Over the course of his career, Eszylfie has earned the Series 6, 63, 65, and 7 licenses, in addition to a life and health insurance license.

Eszylfie began his career at age 22 with New York Life Insurance Company, where he soon ascended to the Chairman's Council, reaching the ranking of #1 Broker in Los Angeles (2006–2013), Chairman's Cabinet, which defines the top 50 agents out of the country's 13,000+ (2010–2013), and #1 Agent for the Company's African–American market (2006–2013). In 2007, he began building his own firm, Taylor Insurance and Financial Services. In 2013, he left New York Life to grow his independent brokerage.

Eszylfie was born and raised in Pasadena, California. As a top-flight high school athlete playing in four varsity sports, he completed a notable collegiate basketball career at Concordia University in Portland, Oregon, graduating magna cum laude with a bachelor's degree in business management.

Eszylfie currently sits on the board of three nonprofit organizations dedicated to business empowerment, children's health, and social services. In his free time, he mentors upcoming youth as the founder of the nonprofit Futures Stars Camp (www.futurestarscamp.org) for kids, which is dedicated to providing basketball training and life coaching skills. In addition to his passion for business, Eszylfie is raising three daughters with his wife in Pasadena, where he still resides.

Vanessa Terzian

818 864-6174 vanessa@vterzianlaw.com

Vanessa Terzian is an adjunct professor of wills and trusts at Southwestern Law School and was named a top attorney of 2016 in *Pasadena Magazine* and named a Rising Star by Super Lawyers. Vanessa began her legal career as a trust administrator for Wells Fargo, N.A. Her experience at Wells Fargo, working closely with clients, portfolio managers, beneficiaries, and other attorneys, shed light on how a poor estate plan can ruin a family's fortune and, more important, their relationships.

After witnessing firsthand the importance of proper planning, Vanessa has pursued her own practice, helping countless families through her expertise in estate and tax planning, asset protection, elder law, kids protection planning, and probate and trust administration. What sets Vanessa apart is her understanding of the needs of growing families, her ability to relate to working parents who desire a better life for themselves and their families, and her know-how to implement strategic estate planning tools in the most cost-efficient and seamless manner. Vanessa also draws on her real estate and business background in crafting comprehensive plans for her clients.

Vanessa is a skilled public speaker, having conducted countless seminars throughout her legal career on various topics of estate planning, including kids protection planning, special needs planning, Medi-Cal planning, advanced tax planning, and asset protection for individuals and small businesses. Vanessa is a faculty member at the Institute for Preparing Heirs.

Vanessa is an active member of the La Canada Flintridge community, where she resides with her husband, Edward, and two sons, Alec and Jack. She is a board member of the Northridge Hospital Foundation and participates in a number of charitable-based organizations. Vanessa has successfully raised thousands of dollars for a variety of charitable causes through fundraising campaigns, which include frequent community-based public-speaking events, charitable dinners, and personal contributions. She believes that the foundation to a successful family unit is care, love, and selflessness and stresses the importance of providing your community with these same tenets that are so essential to your own family's success.

As a family woman, Vanessa understands the importance of protecting your assets, planning for your family's future, and building your own legacy. She takes pride in providing her clients with the sense of comfort and security that comes with having an effective and comprehensive estate plan in place.

Dana Dattola

626 446-6161 danaw@weaverinsurance.com

Dana Dattola is a Certified Insurance Consultant (CIC) and third-generation property and casualty insurance broker. Raised in her family's insurance agency, Dana started helping in the office as a teenager and has been a principal at Weaver & Associates Insurance Brokerage for more than 10 years. After graduating from San Diego State University with a degree in Business Management, Dana returned to her family's insurance brokerage firm where she worked in the personal lines department and eventually transitioned into the commercial lines division. With her flair for facts, continual education and her drive to help her customers, Dana has proven to be one of the top advisors in the insurance industry. Dana acquired the prestigious Certified Insurance Consultant (CIC) designation and is currently pursuing a Certified Risk Management (CIM) designation. Both are nationally recognized professional designations. Dana is proud to be among the top CICs in the Country; "the best and most knowledgeable insurance practitioners in the nation."

What sets Dana and Weaver & Associates apart is their systematic, three-step risk management process designed to increase their customers' profitability by reducing their exposures to loss. Dana specializes in business insurance (workers compensation, general liability, commercial property, and others). The brokerage also provides personal insurance to individuals and business owners (home, auto, umbrella, and others). During her time working on personal insurance lines, she developed a proprietary risk management checklist and policy schedule to help her clients understand their risk exposure and the insurance products they had in place to protect themselves and their families from financial loss.

Weaver & Associates make a point to look at all possible risks and get the best coverage for the least cost to the client.

Dana has always been involved in alternative sports her whole life and placed 1st in Collegiate National water skiing while at SDSU. Born and raised in Los Angeles, California, Dana enjoys her family life with her husband and three children and hopes to continue her family legacy for years to come.

Monty Kennedy

626 765-8163 monty.kennedy@homestreet.com

Monty Kennedy has been in the financial industry for more than 12 years, specializing in mortgage loans since January, 2010. A graduate of Baylor University's Hankamer School of Business, he earned a bachelor's degree in Management and International Business in 2001. Monty prides himself on producing outstanding experiences through developing meaningful relationships with both his clients and business partners. With Monty, you can expect a work ethic and level of professional expertise that far exceeds normal expectations.

In addition to being a certified mortgage planning specialist, Monty has been named a SoCal Region Top Producer and a member of the President's Club by HomeStreet Bank, as well as being named a Five Star Mortgage Professional in 2015. Recipients of the Five Start award represent four percent of mortgage professionals in the Los Angeles area. Clients have considered Monty to be outstanding in his field and have given him high satisfaction ratings, exceeding client expectations time and time again.

Monty currently resides in Pasadena with his wife, the love of his life and college sweetheart, with their three children. Monty is very active in his church where he volunteers in a number of capacities.

Brian Parsons

626 204-3360 brian@theparsonsrealestateteam.com

Brian Parsons began his real estate career in 2006, quickly becoming one of Pasadena's top-producing agents. As a second-generation Realtor, Brian was brought up with a keen understanding of work ethic and putting client's needs before his own. During the past 10 years, he has systematically established himself as one of the most trusted agents in the Pasadena and Los Angeles areas, with extensive experience in new construction projects, first-time home buyers, luxury estates, and everything in between.

Brian was born and raised in the Pasadena area where he still resides. He attended the University of Arizona and went to work for Disney World in Florida shortly after college. Brian oversaw hotel recreation operations, and it was at Disney where he fine-tuned his customer service skills. But there was something missing. The family business was calling him home. His mother, Jayne Parsons, had started her real estate business in 1984 and she needed a partner. Brian returned to Pasadena, California in 2006. His first year back, he was recognized as Keller Williams Realty Pasadena's "Rookie of the Year", outselling every new agent that year.

Brian's ability to excel in one of America's most competitive markets is the result of his constant drive to help others and his local market knowledge. He brings invaluable expertise on a localized level. Brian is consistently ranked as a top producer, not only within the Pasadena area, but within Keller Williams Realty International as a whole. He currently oversees a top-producing team of seven people and is looking to expand operations into other market areas.

Aside from helping more than 600 families with their real estate needs throughout the years, Brian is an avid golfer and enjoys spending time with his wife, Lauren, and their three dogs.

Charles G. Stanislawski, M.B.T., C.P.A., C.T.C.

626 441-0330 chuck@stanislawskiandcompany.com

Chuck Stanislawski has been providing expertise in tax, accounting, and consulting to Stanislawski & Company's clients for more than 30 years. He specializes in many types of businesses, including real estate, manufacturing, and retail. He also has extensive expertise in individual income taxation, estates and trusts, probate accounting, private foundations, and nonprofit organizations.

Chuck launched his career at Deloitte, Haskins and Sells (now Deloitte) in Los Angeles in 1979. There he specialized in financial audits and accounting and tax services for medium to large businesses in a wide variety of industries. In 1985, he purchased Stanislawski & Company from his father who founded the firm more than 50 years ago.

As a popular public speaker, Chuck enjoys speaking at numerous professional groups (for example, Lorman Education Services) and local community organizations. His articles have appeared in various entertainment, business, and real estate publications. He has also been featured on ABC and KTLA regarding current tax developments.

On behalf of Stanislawski & Company, Inc., Chuck has served as a member of the International Society of Certified Public Accountants, the American Institute of Certified Public

Accountants, American Institute of Certified Tax Coaches and the Institute for Preparing Heirs. He has served on the board of numerous organizations, including University of Southern California School of Accounting, Pasadena Museum of History—vice president, CPA Law Forum, Pasadena Civic Auditorium (Emmy Awards)—treasurer, Pasadena Chamber Political Action Committee—treasurer, Pediatric Orthopedic Institute—chairman, Huntington Hospital Planned Giving Advisory Council, South Pasadena Estate and Trust Committee, member of the Archdiocese of Los Angeles Estate & Trust Committee appointed by His Eminence Cardinal Roger Mahony, and member of the Audit Committee for the United States Polo Association. Chuck was also appointed by the mayor as a City of Pasadena commissioner.

Chuck holds a bachelor's degree in accounting and a master's degree in business taxation from the University of Southern California. He is the proud father of three daughters. Besides his family, his next greatest passion is polo. He competes at four local polo clubs and has played internationally.

Made in the USA
San Bernardino, CA
11 January 2018